The Complete Prompt Master Manual

Stelvin Saji

The Complete Prompt Master Manual

Author's Note

The Complete Prompt Master Manual was created with one clear intention: to remove the guesswork from interacting with artificial intelligence. In a world where AI is becoming an essential partner in coding, design, writing, research, and daily productivity, the difference between an average result and an extraordinary one often comes down to a single factor, your prompt.

This manual is built to give you clarity, not confusion. Every prompt, explanation, and guideline inside this book reflects the same principles professionals use to achieve fast, accurate, and consistent outcomes. My goal is to empower you with a toolkit that doesn't just teach you how to prompt, but helps you understand why certain prompts unlock deeper, smarter, and more refined responses from AI. Whether you're a creator, developer, student, or someone exploring the potential of AI for the first time, this book is your map. With it, you'll navigate complex tasks with confidence, communicate with AI more effectively, and unlock results that feel both seamless and intentional.

Thank you for choosing this manual. I hope it becomes a trusted companion in your creative and technical journey, one that elevates your work, sharpens your skills, and helps you harness the full power of AI without trial and error.

Warm Regards,
Stelvin Saji - Author & Editor

Nano Banana Pro Master Prompt Library

A curated collection of high-power prompts for image creation, design, branding, architecture, marketing, and cinematic generation.

These prompts are crafted with precision for AI image generators, incorporating detailed descriptors for composition, lighting, color palettes, textures, and stylistic influences to yield professional-grade results. Each is optimized for depth and accuracy, drawing from real-world photography, design principles, and cinematic techniques.

Contents

Chapter 6: Marketing, Business & Branding Prompts

Chapter 7: Education & Learning Prompts

Chapter 8: Image + Video + Audio Prompts

Chapter 9: Advanced Prompting Techniques

Specialized Prompt Packs

Resources
(Recommended Tools & Extensions)

Gemini API Quick Start

Model Comparison Table (Gemini vs ChatGPT vs Claude vs Llama)

Conclusion

Introduction

In today's fast-moving world of artificial intelligence, tools like large language models (LLMs) are becoming the engines behind creativity, productivity, and problem-solving. Among them, Google Gemini has quickly risen to the top not just as another model, but as a major leap forward. With the release of Gemini 3, Google's most advanced multimodal AI, the limits of what AI can do have expanded once again.

Mastering Gemini: Advanced Prompt Engineering for the Next Generation of AI is designed to help beginners understand and use this technology with confidence. You don't need any technical background. If you're curious, creative, and ready to explore, this book will guide you step by step. Prompt engineering is simply the skill of giving AI clear, effective instructions. Think of it like having a conversation where your words shape the results you get. Good prompts lead to accurate, useful answers; unclear prompts can lead to confusing or incorrect outputs. And as AI becomes a part of everyday life helping with writing, research, coding, design, and more learning how to communicate with it has become essential.

Gemini stands out because it was built from the beginning to work across many formats at once: text, images, audio, video, and even code. This means you can ask it to analyze a picture, summarize a document, and generate code all in one seamless interaction. That level of reasoning and flexibility is what makes Gemini 3 such a powerful tool. This book is structured to help you grow from the basics to more advanced techniques. Early chapters introduce core concepts, middle sections teach practical prompting skills, and later chapters explores deeper topics like implementing Gemini API in your code. Along the way, you'll find some tips so you can learn by doing.

Q. Why does this matter now?

In 2025 & beyond, AI adoption has exploded. Gemini 3 is outperforming most major models including ChatGPT 5.1 in reasoning, coding, and multimodal tasks. It's also integrated into tools people use every day, like Google Workspace and Search, making it easier than ever to apply prompt engineering in real life.By the end of this book, you'll know how to talk to AI Models clearly, creatively, and effectively. Whether you're a student, a developer, a designer, a marketer, or simply someone exploring AI for the first time, this book will help you unlock the full potential of the world's most advanced AI system.

Let's begin the journey one prompt at a time.

Q. What Makes Gemini Different?

To understand why Gemini stands out, it helps to see how it compares to other major AI models. By late 2025, the AI world is filled with powerful systems like ChatGPT 5.1, Claude 3.5, and Llama 3.1. Each of them is great at something ChatGPT is strong in creative writing, Claude is thoughtful and ethical, and Llama is popular with developers who like to customize models.

Gemini 3, however, feels different. It combines three major strengths that make it especially helpful for beginners:

1. True multimodality
2. Strong reasoning abilities
3. Smooth integration with Google's ecosystem

These strengths give users simple, accurate, and complete results even from basic prompts.

Gemini 3's first major strength lies in its native multimodality, which simply means it understands different types of information text, images, audio, video, and even code as one interconnected system. Earlier AI models were built mainly for text and had additional features bolted on later, which made tasks involving multiple formats feel clunky or inconsistent. Gemini, on the other hand, was designed from the ground up to treat all these formats as part of a single language. This gives it a unique ability to move smoothly between them. Tthis feels incredibly natural: you can upload an image, ask a question about it, include some text, and request an analysis all in one prompt. If you upload something like an ultrasound scan and ask Gemini to explain the findings in simple, patient-friendly language based on current cardiology guidelines, it doesn't just describe the image it interprets it in context, connects it to relevant medical information, and produces a cohesive explanation. This integrated approach is especially meaningful for students, creators, researchers, healthcare learners, and anyone working across visual and textual content.

Another area where Gemini stands out is its reasoning ability. Gemini 3 is designed to break down complex tasks into smaller, logical steps before producing an answer. Even though it doesn't show every step unless asked, its internal reasoning is structured and deliberate, allowing it to handle multi-step problems in math, coding, logic, and analysis with remarkable accuracy. For example, when you ask it to debug a Python script and explain how to fix edge cases, it doesn't just correct the code it also walks you through the logic in a straightforward way, helping you understand why the fix works. This makes Gemini especially valuable as a learning partner. Compared to other models, ChatGPT often feels more conversational, while Claude is known for its empathetic tone. Gemini takes a different approach: it responds with clarity, precision, and factual grounding, making it feel like an analytical assistant that prioritizes accuracy over emotion. Seeking reliable answers and clear explanations, this can be incredibly reassuring.

Gemini's third major advantage is its deep integration with Google's ecosystem, which makes practical, real-world tasks easier and more seamless. Since it connects directly with tools like Google Search, Google Docs, Google Sheets, Drive, and Vertex AI, it can perform actions that other models simply can't do natively.

For instance, if you ask, "Find Alphabet's Q3 earnings, summarize the results, and create a chart in Google Sheets," Gemini can pull the data from Search, verify it, summarize it, and generate a ready-to-use chart all within the same workflow.

This kind of real-time access reduces the risk of hallucinations because Gemini grounds its responses in live, verifiable information. Another advantage is accessibility: Gemini Advanced is priced affordably and offers higher usage limits than many competitors, which lowers the barrier for beginners who want to explore without worrying about running out of tokens or paying premium fees.

Of course, Gemini isn't perfect. It comes with a few small quirks that you should be aware of. The model tends to prefer short, clear, and direct prompts rather than long, descriptive ones. A style that might work well with ChatGPT may not feel as effective with Gemini because Gemini responds best when you get straight to the point. In creative writing, Claude still has an edge it produces emotional, poetic, and character-driven narratives more naturally. Meanwhile, Llama remains the favorite among developers who prefer open-source tools they can customize. Gemini takes a more controlled approach to training and deployment, which improves safety but limits flexibility in some highly technical customization scenarios. These quirks don't diminish its power they simply help you understand how to communicate with it more effectively.

What makes Gemini especially appealing for beginners is how empowering it feels from the very first interaction. Even without prior experience, you can achieve advanced results with surprisingly simple prompts. You can upload a rough sketch and ask Gemini to turn it into functioning code. You can feed it a melody and request musical variations. You can give it two complex policies and ask for a clear comparison in plain language. You can upload a long video and ask for a step-by-step explanation of everything happening in it. Instead of forcing you to understand complicated technical concepts before getting meaningful results, Gemini meets you where you are and lifts you higher. It simplifies complex ideas, handles multi-step problems gracefully, and encourages you to experiment without fear of making mistakes.

In many ways, Gemini turns beginners into confident creators by making advanced AI feel approachable, intuitive, and powerful from day one.

Q. How to use this Book?

Complete Prompt Master is built for everyone, whether you're just starting or you're a professional looking to refine your craft. This book gives you clear, practical prompts and techniques so you can get the best results from AI, every time.

1. For Beginners

If you're new to prompting, think of this as your roadmap. You'll learn how to:

- Ask clear, effective questions
- Structure prompts for accurate results
- Experiment confidently
- Apply prompts across coding, design, writing, creativity, and more

Everything is written simply so you can learn fast and start using AI with confidence.

2. For Professionals

If you already work with AI or use it in your field, this book becomes a productivity tool. Inside, you'll find:

- Precision prompts for technical, creative, and business tasks
- Frameworks you can reuse in your daily workflow
- Strategies to polish, accelerate, and scale your output

These prompts help you work smarter and produce professional-quality results consistently.

Use the prompts in this book actively!. Copy them, adapt them, and try them out. Experiment with different tones and styles to match your needs, and save the prompts you rely on most. As you grow, revisit various sections; you'll find that your results improve each time. Even spending just a few minutes with this book can sharpen your thinking and elevate your prompting skills.

Converting Prompts for ChatGPT, Claude & Llama

This section is for anyone who wants their prompts to work across different AI models, not just Gemini. Each model has its own style, strengths, and quirks, so a prompt that works well for one may not perform the same on another. ChatGPT tends to be creative and descriptive, Claude is thoughtful and empathetic, and Llama works best when instructions are very clear and structured. Gemini prefers short, precise prompts unless you specifically ask for detail. By understanding these differences, you can quickly adjust a prompt so it produces strong results no matter which model you use.

The easiest way to convert a prompt is to follow four simple steps:

1. Diagnose
2. Deconstruct
3. Rebuild
4. Validate

First, diagnose the prompt by noticing which model it was originally written for and what that model naturally emphasizes. Next, deconstruct the prompt by breaking it into four basic parts: the intent (what you want), the context (any background), the constraints (rules like tone or length), and the output format. Once you have the bare essentials, you can rebuild it in the style that Gemini or any other model understands clearly. For example, a creative ChatGPT prompt might need clearer structure, a specific role, or numbered instructions to work well in Gemini. A Claude-style prompt might need less emotional padding. A Llama-style prompt might need more examples or step-by-step cues. After rewriting the prompt, validate it by testing it in each model and comparing the results. Check whether the output is on-topic, clear, and efficient. If a model gives too little detail, you can add small instructions like "Give three vivid examples."

Source Model	Key Trait	Conversion Heuristic for Gemini	Example Adaptation
ChatGPT	Creative fluency	Add structure using numbered steps or specific formats to keep responses focused	**Original:** "Brainstorm 10 ideas" **Gemini-adapted:** "List 10 ranked ideas with pros and cons in bullet points"
Claude	Empathetic verbosity	Condense into direct instructions and clearly specify tone	**Original:** "Discuss pros/cons thoughtfully" **Gemini-adapted:** "Outline pros and cons in a 200-word balanced report"
Llama	Modular efficiency	Include examples and explicit constraints to provide depth	**Original:** "Classify sentiments" **Gemini-adapted:** "Classify sentiments using 2-shot examples; output results in JSON format"

If a model rambles too much, shorten the instructions or use bullet points. If a model needs more clarity, add extra context or a simple example. With practice, you'll naturally learn how to adjust prompts for different AIs. This makes your skills more flexible and ensures your prompts work well anywhere whether you're using ChatGPT, Claude, Llama, or Gemini.

In practice, converting prompts across different models is less about strict rules and more about understanding the underlying intent treat it as an art of finding equivalence, not exact matches. For beginners, start small: try adapting five to ten prompts each week, and over time, you'll naturally develop an intuitive sense of how to translate ideas between models. Within Gemini's ecosystem, this skill becomes even more powerful. You can export your adapted prompts to Google Workspace for collaborative editing and refinement, making it easy to share and improve ideas with others.

By mastering this approach, you're not just writing prompts you're learning to orchestrate AI across multiple platforms, turning each model's strengths into a harmonious, productive workflow.

Chapter 1 Prompting Fundamentals

In the collaboration between human creativity and artificial intelligence, prompting is like the conductor's baton it guides the vast capabilities of large language models (LLMs) like Gemini 3 toward useful and insightful outcomes. By December 2025, Gemini 3's advanced reasoning engine allows it to respond to multimodal queries almost instantly, making the ability to craft effective prompts a key skill for any beginner. This chapter focuses on the fundamentals of prompting, helping you understand not just what to ask, but how to ask it so that Gemini can interpret your intent precisely. Prompts are more than simple queries they are carefully structured instructions that shape the model's responses, reducing randomness and amplifying meaningful output.

Q. What Is a Prompt?

A prompt is the interface between your intention and the AI's reasoning. It's the input you provide that guides the model's generative process. For Gemini 3, a prompt isn't limited to text—it can include images, audio, or code, all integrated seamlessly into a single request. Unlike a basic search query, which retrieves information, a prompt instructs the model to generate content, drawing from patterns and knowledge learned during training. You can think of a prompt as a lens: it takes a broad or vague idea and focuses it into a clear, actionable instruction. For example, a beginner might ask, "Tell me about climate change," which may result in a generic or scattered answer. A more refined prompt would be: "As a climatologist synthesizing IPCC AR7 findings, outline three adaptive strategies for urban resilience in megacities, formatted as a policy brief with measurable metrics." This type of prompt includes a role (climatologist), context (IPCC AR7), constraints (three strategies), and format (policy brief), helping the model provide a precise, high-quality response. Gemini's multimodal capabilities take prompting even further. For instance, you could upload a satellite image of Arctic ice melt and ask, "Extrapolate sea-level rise trajectories from this Landsat-9 image, integrating NOAA 2025 projections," and Gemini will reason across text and visual data to produce a coherent, evidence-based forecast. This demonstrates how prompts can leverage the model's cross-modal reasoning to produce outputs that go beyond simple text generation.

Finally, prompting is an iterative process. Gemini supports self-refinement through meta-prompts like, "Critique your previous response for logical gaps," which allows it to improve its own answers. Beginners should start with zero-shot prompts simple, task-focused instructions and gradually explore few-shot prompts, where examples guide the model's behavior. Well-crafted prompts can dramatically improve accuracy and relevance; in 2025 benchmarks, careful prompt design increased Gemini's MMLU scores from 88% to 94%, rivaling expert human performance in many domains. In short, a prompt is not just a question it is a precise vector of intention that directs the model to deliver meaningful, reliable, and actionable outputs.

Elements of a High-Quality Prompt

Creating a high-quality prompt is less about fancy tricks and more about understanding a few core elements that guide an AI like Gemini toward clear, accurate, and useful responses. Think of a good prompt as a well-structured instruction that helps the model understand exactly what you want. In practice, strong prompts are built around five key elements:

1. Clarity
2. Context
3. Constraints
4. Examples
5. Format

These elements work together to give Gemini the right direction while minimizing confusion.

Clarity means using simple, unambiguous language. If a word can have multiple meanings like "bank" specify what you mean to avoid misunderstandings.

Context sets the stage by telling the model where the information should come from or how it should think about the topic, such as "Using insights from recent climate reports…" This helps the model stay current and relevant.

Constraints define the boundaries: word limits, required tones, safety instructions, or special conditions like "Keep it under 200 words" or "Follow accessibility guidelines." These limits help control the output.

Examples (few-shot prompting) give the AI a pattern to follow, which can significantly improve responses especially for creative or structured tasks.

And finally, format tells Gemini how to present the answer: as a list, a table, a JSON object, a paragraph, or any other structure you need. When combined, these five elements transform a vague request into a precise instruction, resulting in much better responses.

Role, Tone & Output Control

Role, tone, and output control are the three main tools that help you shape how an AI responds. Think of them as giving the model a personality, a mood, and a clear set of instructions. When you assign a role for example, "You are a friendly teacher" or "Explain this like Sherlock Holmes", you guide the AI into behaving like that character.

This works because modern models, especially Gemini 3, are trained on a huge variety of conversations and can easily adapt their style when you set a clear persona. Even a simple question like "Explain blockchain" becomes far more engaging when paired with a role such as "Explain blockchain as if you were Satoshi Nakamoto talking to beginners." The tone shapes the emotional feel of the answer. You can make the AI sound professional, casual, dramatic, humorous, poetic, or motivational by saying things like "Use an encouraging tone," or "Write in a simple, calm style." These tone instructions help beginners control the mood and clarity of the response.

Finally, output control lets you decide exactly how the answer should look. You can specify length ("Keep it under 150 words"), structure ("Write it in three sections"), format ("Use bullet points"), or detail level ("Explain step-by-step"). You can even ask for citations, summaries, tables, or creative formats. All three elements role, tone, and output work together to help beginners create clear, powerful, and predictable prompts. When used well, they transform the AI from a general assistant into a customized guide that matches exactly what you need.

Using System Instructions in Gemini

System instructions in Gemini act like the "master rules" that guide how the model behaves across all interactions. Unlike normal prompts which only affect the current message system instructions stay active in the background until you change them, making them incredibly useful for beginners who want consistent results. You can think of them like the foundation of a house: once set, everything you build on top follows those rules automatically.

In Gemini 3 (as of December 2025), system instructions are built directly into the API for apps made with Firebase, Vertex AI, or Next.js SDKs. They allow you to define the model's personality, priorities, and communication style without repeating instructions every time. For example, you can force the model to always be concise, always think step-by-step, or always behave like a mentor. Setting them in JavaScript is simple. In the Gemini JavaScript SDK, you can do something like:

```
import { GoogleGenerativeAI } from "@google/generative-ai";

const genAI = new GoogleGenerativeAI({
  apiKey: process.env.GEMINI_API_KEY,
  systemInstruction: "Respond clearly and simply. Prioritize accuracy over creativity."
});

const model = genAI.getGenerativeModel({ model: "gemini-3.0-pro" });

const result = await model.generateContent("Explain quantum computing for beginners.");
console.log(result.response.text());
);
```

This code connects your project to Google's Gemini AI and tells it how you want it to behave every time it answers. First, it imports the GoogleGenerativeAI class so you can use the Gemini models inside your JavaScript or TypeScript project. Then it creates a new Gemini client using your API key, which proves that your app is allowed to use the model. While creating this client, you also provide a system instruction a permanent rule that guides the model's personality and style. In this case, you're telling Gemini to "respond clearly and simply" and to "prioritize accuracy over creativity," which means every answer it generates will follow this tone unless you change it. After that, the code selects the specific

AI model you want to use (gemini-3.0-pro). Then it sends a prompt "Explain quantum computing for beginners" and waits for the AI to generate a response. Finally, it prints the text of the AI's answer to the console. In simple terms, this code sets the model's behavior, sends it a question, and displays the answer.

```
import { GoogleGenerativeAI } from "@google/generative-ai";
import { NextRequest, NextResponse } from "next/server";

const client = new GoogleGenerativeAI({
  apiKey: process.env.GEMINI_API_KEY!,
  systemInstruction: "Act like a collaborative tutor. Ask clarifying questions when needed."
});

export async function POST(req: NextRequest) {
  try {
    const { prompt }: { prompt: string } = await req.json();

    const model = client.getGenerativeModel({
      model: "gemini-3.0-pro"
    });

    const result = await model.generateContent(prompt);
    const text = result.response.text();

    return NextResponse.json({ output: text });
  } catch (error) {
    console.error("Gemini API Error:", error);
    return NextResponse.json({ error: "Something went wrong." }, { status: 500 });
  }
}
```

In the NextJS version, it creates an API endpoint in Next.js that allows your app to send prompts to Google's Gemini 3.0 Pro model and receive AI-generated responses. It starts by importing the Gemini SDK and the Next.js request/response helpers, then creates a Gemini client using your API key so the system knows who you are and that you have permission to access the model. At the same time, it sets a system instruction a long-term rule telling the model to act like a helpful tutor and ask clarifying questions when needed. Inside the POST function, the server receives a request, reads the JSON body, and extracts a prompt string sent by the user. It then selects the Gemini model you want to use (gemini-3.0-pro) and sends the prompt to it. Gemini processes the prompt, generates a response, and the code extracts the final text output. That text is then returned to the client as JSON so your frontend can display it.

A try/catch block is included to prevent crashes if anything goes wrong, the API returns a clean error message instead of breaking the server. In short, this file acts as a bridge between your frontend and Gemini: it receives a prompt, sends it to the model, gets the answer, and returns it safely.

Common Prompting Mistakes to Avoid

When beginners start prompting, it's common to run into a few mistakes that weaken the quality of Gemini's responses. One of the biggest issues is being too vague for example, asking "Give me marketing ideas" usually leads to generic answers because the model has nothing specific to work with. A stronger approach is to add details like goals, audience, style, or format.

Another frequent mistake is not giving enough context. Without background information, Gemini may fill gaps on its own, which increases the chance of inaccuracies or hallucinated details. On the opposite side, some users make the mistake of overloading the prompt with too much text, which can confuse the model and bury the important parts of the request. Keeping instructions focused and clear works best.Beginners also forget to specify the output format if you want bullets, a table, or JSON, you must say so; otherwise the response may come back in long paragraphs you didn't expect.

Finally, there's session confusion, where users keep prompting without resetting or guiding the model, causing it to carry irrelevant info from earlier messages. Starting a new thread or telling the model "Ignore previous instructions" helps keep things clean. By avoiding vagueness, adding meaningful context, keeping prompts concise, being clear about format, and maintaining session clarity, beginners can reliably get better, more accurate, and more useful results from Gemini.

Chapter 2 Productivity & Everyday Life Prompts

In our busy, fast-moving lives, it's easy to feel overwhelmed by tasks, responsibilities, and constant digital noise. AI tools like Gemini can help bring back clarity and control by taking care of everyday tasks more efficiently. By late 2025, Gemini 3 had become deeply integrated into Google Workspace, and many users reported feeling significantly more productive because it could help with planning, writing, organizing information, and simplifying decisions.

This chapter is designed to show beginners how to use AI not just as a fun tool, but as a practical partner that supports your daily routines. Instead of giving quick, shallow tips, we focus on meaningful prompts that you can actually use to manage tasks, think creatively, summarize notes, write emails, plan your day, and even research new topics. You'll explore six key areas of productivity, and each one includes a short explanation followed by ten ready-to-use prompts 60 in total that are crafted with clarity, structure, and purpose.

As you use them, feel free to tweak the wording, ask the model to improve its own responses, or request a different format. The goal is to help you build a smoother, more intentional daily rhythm, with AI acting as a helpful companion that reduces stress and frees up your time for what truly matters.

1. Task Management

Task management is one of the most important skills for staying organized and productive, especially in a world where constant notifications and distractions make it hard to focus. Instead of letting tasks pile up or guessing what to do next, you can use AI to break everything down into clear, manageable steps. Whether you're organizing your day with the Eisenhower Matrix (which helps you separate urgent tasks from important ones) or using the GTD (Getting Things Done) method to clean up scattered notes and ideas, AI can guide you through each step. These prompts act like a digital assistant that helps you prioritize, plan ahead, and stay on track reducing the mental load and saving you time.

With a bit of practice, AI becomes a helpful partner that turns overwhelming to-do lists into simple, actionable plans, helping you stay focused and in control throughout your day.

Prompts :

1. Eisenhower Matrix Organizer:

"Act as a productivity expert familiar with Stephen Covey's methods. Take these tasks [list 5-10 tasks] and sort them into an Eisenhower Matrix: Urgent and Important, Urgent but Not Important, Important but Not Urgent, and Neither. For each task, give a priority score from 1-3, suggest if it can be delegated, and include estimated time needed plus possible obstacles. Present it in a markdown table."

2. GTD Capture and Clarify Process:

"Follow David Allen's Getting Things Done (GTD) approach: Start by capturing these raw ideas or notes [paste your unfiltered tasks/ notes]. Then, clarify each one into a clear next action, a deferral, or something to archive. Structure the output like this: Bullet 1: The original item; Bullet 2: The action or outcome; Bullet 3: How often to review it (daily or weekly). Keep the total under 200 words."

3. Pomodoro Session Planner:

"Create a 4-round Pomodoro plan for [describe your project, e.g., 'writing a 2,000-word report']. Each round is 25 minutes of focused work, with 5-minute breaks including quick resets like deep breathing. Add a 15-minute review at the end. Format it as a timeline table, factoring in your natural energy highs based on daily rhythms."

4. Task Dependency Mapper:

"Think like a project manager and map out these connected tasks [list them] as a simple dependency graph (like a DAG no loops). Highlight the critical path, any bottlenecks, and tasks that can run in parallel. Output an ASCII art diagram, followed by a bulleted list of ways to address issues, inspired by agile team reviews."

5. Energy-Based Scheduler:

"Based on my energy patterns [describe them, e.g., 'I'm sharp from 9 AM to noon but crash after lunch'], reschedule these tasks [list them] to match my natural cycles. Suggest calendar blocks with 10-15 minute buffers for switching gears, and prioritize the top 20% of tasks that deliver 80% of the value using the Pareto principle."

6. Task Review and Improvement Guide:

"Review these finished tasks [list what happened]: What went smoothly? Where were the hurdles? Create 3 improved prompts for next time, organized in a SWOT table (Strengths, Weaknesses, Opportunities, Threats), with tips from kaizen for small, ongoing tweaks."

7. Task Batching Expert:

"Group these varied tasks [list them] into batches by type (like creative work or admin chores) to cut down on mental switches. Recommend time lengths for each batch, tools like Notion templates, and simple rituals to shift between them. Output numbered batches with why they work and rough ROI estimates."

8. Risk-Aware Task Predictor:

"Pretend you're running a quick Monte Carlo simulation: For these tasks [list with deadlines], estimate completion chances in three scenarios—realistic, best-case, and worst-case. Factor in task links with basic probabilities. Show it as a text-based Gantt chart with built-in buffers for surprises."

9. Habit Stacking Planner:

"Use BJ Fogg's habit stacking to weave these new tasks [list them] into your daily routines attach them to triggers like 'right after my morning coffee.' Build a 7-day starter plan in calendar format, including check-ins and tips to make it stick long-term."

10. Kanban Board Simulator:

"Turn these tasks [list them] into a Kanban setup: Columns for To-Do, In-Progress (limit to 3 items max), and Done. Add rough time estimates for each and flags for slowdowns. Display it as a text board with predictions on your overall speed."

2. Brainstorming

Brainstorming is the stage where fresh ideas begin to unfold, helping you step outside your usual way of thinking and explore new possibilities. Today, AI makes this process even faster and more effective recent studies show that it can boost innovation efforts by nearly 30%, giving you a real advantage when generating solutions or creative concepts. These prompts are designed to guide you through approachable frameworks like SCAMPER and the Six Thinking Hats, which break down creativity into simple steps anyone can follow. Whether you're completely new to brainstorming or just looking for a clearer path, these tools help transform loose, imaginative thoughts into ideas that feel practical, achievable, and exciting to build on.

Prompts :

1. SCAMPER Idea Generator:

"Use the SCAMPER technique (Substitute, Combine, Adapt, Modify, Put to other uses, Eliminate, Reverse) on [your main idea, e.g., 'an urban mobility app']. Come up with one variation for each letter, rate its feasibility (1-10), and note who it might appeal to. Output as a text-based mind map with branches."

2. Six Thinking Hats Session:

"Apply Edward de Bono's Six Thinking Hats to [your topic, e.g., 'sustainable packaging']: Go through White (facts), Red (gut feelings), Black (risks), Yellow (upsides), Green (new ideas), and Blue (overview). Wrap up with a table of the top 3 combined ideas."

3. Analogy-Based Idea Mixer:

"Draw analogies from unrelated areas [e.g., 'ant colonies or jazz bands'] to inspire solutions for [your focus, e.g., 'e-commerce shipping']. Brainstorm 5 fresh mixes, each with a quick prototype idea and questions to test it."

4. Reverse Brainstorming Flip:

"Flip the script: Brainstorm ways to make [your goal, e.g., 'better team collaboration'] worse. Pick the top 3 'bad' ideas and turn them into positive fixes. Format: Original problem > Worsening tactics > Reversed solutions (in bullets)."

5. Persona-Led Idea Storm:

"Imagine three user types [e.g., busy parent, tech enthusiast, busy executive] tackling [your challenge]. Get 4 bold ideas from each, then rank them using a simple scoring grid. Output by persona, ending with a summary 'heatmap' of winners."

6. Trend and Industry Mashup:

"Blend [a hot trend, e.g., 'Web3 tech'] with [a traditional field, e.g., 'real estate']. Spot early signals and drivers to create 6 forward-thinking ideas, ranked by potential disruption and ethical fit."

7. Crazy Constraints Brainstorm:

"Add fun limits to [your open topic, e.g., 'home workout tools']: Under $5, only recycled materials, and celebrate mistakes. From the mess, pull out 4 realistic ideas with basic business outlines."

8. Expert Roundtable Simulation:

"Role-play a discussion among four pros (designer, engineer, marketer, ethicist) on [your idea starter]. Write out their back-and-forth, then summarize into a pitch outline with quick SWOT notes."

9. Metaphor Idea Builder:

"Turn [your need, e.g., 'building emotional strength during tough times'] into a metaphor [e.g., 'a city survival kit']. Brainstorm 5 parts of the 'kit,' translating each from image to real steps with a simple plan."

10. Morphological Idea Grid:

"Build a 3x3 grid for [your innovation area, e.g., 'personal finance apps']: Rows for features like interface (app, web, voice); columns for mechanics (gamified, AI-driven, predictive). Fill each box with a hybrid concept, scored for originality and ease to scale."

3. Note Summaries

Summarizing notes helps you turn overwhelming information into clear, meaningful points you can actually remember and use. In a world where the average worker faces nearly 150GB of data every week, it's easy to feel lost or overloaded. That's why these prompts focus on approachable methods like the Pyramid Principle and TL;DR summaries. They guide you to sort through messy notes, highlight what truly matters, and express it in a way that's short, structured, and easy to understand. Whether you're studying, working, or organizing your thoughts, these techniques make the process feel manageable and help you build strong habits for learning and productivity.

Prompts :

1. Pyramid Summary Builder:

"Use Barbara Minto's Pyramid Principle to summarize these notes [paste them]: Lead with the main idea, then 3-5 supporting points with evidence. Output in nested bullets, under 300 words, and flag any open questions."

2. Quick TL;DR with Actions:

"Boil down [your notes] to a 150-word TL;DR: Main point, 3 key takeaways, and 2 next steps. Explain it simply like you're teaching a friend (Feynman style), plus a text outline like a mind map."

3. Theme-Based Note Cluster:

"Group [your notes] into 4 natural themes using affinity mapping. For each: A short summary paragraph, standout quotes, and what it means overall. Use sections with links between themes and notes on missing pieces."

4. Q&A Note Rephrase:

"Rewrite [your notes] as 5 question-and-answer pairs: Question from the notes > Supporting evidence > Balanced response. Build from basic to deeper, ending with a big-picture question to explore next."

5. Executive Summary with Mood Check:

"Create a 100-word neutral overview of [your notes], then trace the emotional flow (ups and downs) like a sentiment analysis. Add a table of 3 decisions to make, with pros and cons."

6. Timeline Story from Notes:

"Connect [scattered notes] into a logical timeline story: Key events, how they link, and hints of what's next. Keep it to 250 words, with a simple ASCII timeline and spotted patterns."

7. Summary with Smart Guesses:

"Summarize [your notes], spotting 2-3 logical holes and filling them with reasonable guesses based on the info. Output: Main summary > Identified gaps > Suggested fixes > Confidence level (low/medium/high) for each."

8. Multi-View Note Lens:

"View [your notes] from three angles (optimist, critic, visionary): 50 words per view. Then, overlap them in a text Venn diagram, noting shared ideas and conflicts."

9. Flashcard Creator from Notes:

"Make 8 flashcards from [your notes] in Anki style: Front (question or term), Back (short explanation + memory trick). Group by easy/medium/hard, with tips for review spacing."

10. Story Arc Condenser: "

Shape [your notes] into a 3-part story: Setup (background), Conflict (main issues), Resolution (key lessons). Use engaging language for recall; 200 words max, bolding repeated themes."

4. Email Writing

Emails are one of the most important ways we communicate at work, but managing them can feel overwhelming—especially when an average inbox receives hundreds of messages a day. These prompts are designed to help you write emails that are clear, confident, and effective, even if you're still building your professional communication skills. They draw inspiration from proven persuasive techniques, like those shared by Robert Cialdini, to help you express your ideas in a way that feels natural and respectful while still getting results. Whether you're reaching out to a colleague, asking for help, sharing an update, or pitching an idea, these prompts show you how to stay brief, stay focused, and sound professional without overthinking every sentence. This makes email writing less stressful and much more impactful.

Prompts :

1. Cold Pitch Email Drafter:

"Write a cold email to [target, e.g., 'a venture capitalist'] about [your idea]: Start with their specific challenge, build interest with AIDA (Attention, Interest, Desire, Action), and end with a small ask. Keep it confident and team-oriented, under 150 words."

2. Smart Follow-Up Editor:

"Polish this email draft [paste it] for someone who hasn't replied: Add a free tip (reciprocity), a deadline nudge (scarcity), and a quick success story (social proof). Show the changes with reasons why."

3. Feedback Request Email:

"Draft an email asking [team or boss] for project feedback: Start with thanks, use 3 open questions based on SBI (Situation, Behavior, Impact). End warmly and gratefully; keep it professional but friendly."

4. Salary Negotiation Responder:

"Reply to [this offer, e.g., 'base salary of $80K']: Start high with industry benchmarks, give on smaller points, and suggest mutual wins. Structure: Show understanding > State your case > Team up; max 120 words."

5. Crisis Response Email:

"Write a fix-it email for [situation, e.g., 'a late project deadline']: Take full responsibility, share your recovery steps, and rebuild confidence with openness. Tone: Caring but firm, with a sincere apology."

6. Networking Follow-Up:

"Craft a follow-up email after connecting on LinkedIn: Mention your shared interest, share a tailored resource, and suggest an easy next chat. Keep it to 100 words, with a P.S. for extra spark."

7. Report Update Email:

"Turn [main report highlights] into a quick email for stakeholders: Short intro, 3 data points with chart ideas, and questions for next steps. Make it story-like with bullets for skimmability."

8. New Hire Welcome:

"Write a welcome email for [new team member]: Share 4 fast-start tips, a bit on company culture, and your contact as a guide. Add excitement through a short welcome story; mention easy resources."

9. Graceful Decline Email:

"Decline [offer or invite, e.g., 'a conference speaking slot'] politely: Thank them sincerely, explain your limits gently, and leave the door open. End warmly; under 80 words."

10. Advocacy Push Email:

"Build an email to [key person, e.g., 'a policy advisor'] supporting [cause]: Mix your expertise (ethos), a personal tale (pathos), and facts (logos). End with one clear action; urgent but polite, 140 words max."

5. Research Assistance

Research can feel overwhelming, especially with the massive amount of information produced every day. It's easy to get lost or not know where to start. These prompts are designed to act like a helpful guide, teaching you how to search smarter instead of harder. They encourage you to use simple retrieval techniques, ask the right questions, and think critically about what you find. Instead of just collecting random facts, you learn how to connect ideas, compare sources, and pull out the information that actually matters. This makes research feel less like a confusing maze and more like a clear, step-by-step process. For beginners, it's a great way to build confidence and develop strong research habits without feeling overwhelmed.

Prompts :

1. Literature Review Quickstart:

"Pull together a review on [topic, e.g., 'quantum-safe encryption']: Pick 5 key papers from after 2023, group by themes, and note gaps like a snowball search. Output an annotated list with a connecting summary paragraph."

2. Hypothesis Builder and Tester:

"From [your research question], create 3 testable ideas that can be proven wrong (Popper style). Suggest simple tests (variables and measures). Format: Hypothesis > Test plan > Possible results in a table."

3. What-If History Explorer:

"Imagine alternate paths for [event, e.g., 'world without COVID lockdowns']: Map cause-effect chains and odds using basic probability. 200 words, ranking 3 big changes by influence."

4. Source Checker Tool:

"Check these sources [list links or summaries] for trustworthiness with the CRAAP test (Currency, Relevance, Authority, Accuracy, Purpose). Score each 1-10 and suggest what to keep or skip."

5. Cross-Field Connector:

"Link [main area, e.g., 'brain science'] to [related one, e.g., 'AI rules']: Find 4 overlap spots, key examples, and new questions. Show as a text mind map with source hints."

6. Data Blend Helper:

"Combine these data bits [describe or paste] on [theme]: Spot links with stats, suggest charts like heatmaps, and warn on assumptions. Outline like a dashboard summary."

7. Ethics Guide for Research:

"For [your study idea, e.g., 'gene editing experiments'], outline conflicts using core ethics rules (Beauchamp-Childress). Suggest fixes for review boards; format as a pro-con debate."

8. Future Trend Projector:

"Project [trend, e.g., 'brain-like chips'] to 2030: List drivers, surprises, and three scenarios (likely, ideal, tough). View through STEEPV (Social, Tech, Economic, Environment, Political, Values)."

9. Search Query Sharpener:

"Take this vague query [paste it] and break it into 5 deeper ones: Add AND/OR/NOT, filters for dates or types. Give ready search strings for tools like Google Scholar."

10. Simple Meta-Analysis:

"Do a quick overview of [niche, e.g., 'fixing AI biases']: Pull effect strengths from 4-6 studies, describe a text 'forest plot,' and note variations."

6. Personal Planning & Calendar Prompts

Personal planning is all about organizing your time and setting clear goals to stay focused and avoid stress or burnout, which affects a large majority of professionals. These prompts help beginners turn abstract aspirations into concrete, manageable plans. By using frameworks like OKRs (Objectives and Key Results) or principles from habit science, they guide you in breaking down goals into daily, weekly, and monthly actions. You learn how to balance work, learning, and personal growth, while building routines that stick. Instead of feeling overwhelmed by a long to-do list, these prompts help you prioritize, track progress, and adjust your schedule for maximum impact. For beginners, this approach turns personal planning into a structured, actionable process, making self-improvement achievable and sustainable.

Prompts :

1. OKR Goal Setter:

"Build Q1 OKRs from [your aims, e.g., 'shift to AI ethics work']: 3 big goals (motivating), 4-5 measurable results each. Tie to your values; output as a table ready for Google Sheets."

2. Body-Rhythm Calendar:

"Fit [your weekly routine] to natural cycles like sleep peaks or energy dips: Slot tough tasks in high-energy windows, add rest after lows, plus food and exercise ties. Show as a text weekly grid."

3. Time Use Value Check:

"Review [last week's log] against [your top 5 values]: Spot 80/20 mismatches, suggest swaps. Output: Table of findings > Plan to fix with routine ties."

4. Backup Plan Builder:

"For [goal, e.g., 'prep for a talk'], make a main plan plus 2 backups (e.g., for tech glitches). Timeline with checks; add a risk grid at the end."

5. Weekly Reflection Setup:

"Create a reflection routine: 3 questions (wins, lessons, tweaks) with Stoic twists. Slot it in your week, with a bullet template for tracking."

6. Boundary Protector Calendar:

"Tweak [your schedule draft] for better balance: Add fun buffers and no-meeting zones. Include sample replies for pushy requests; show updated outline like a calendar export."

7. Long-Term Vision Backtrack:

"From [5-year dream, e.g., 'lead in tech'], work backward to quarterly steps. Output: Dream story > Step ladder > Ways to stay accountable."

8. Tiny Habit Chain: "Break [big goal, e.g., 'train for a half-marathon'] into 21 days of small steps: Use cue-action-reward (Duhigg style). Show a sample daily plan."

9. Calendar Flow Booster:

"Clean up [busy schedule] for more magic moments: Group similar items, cut duplicates, add open slots for ideas. Report changes with before/after notes."

10. No-Regrets Decision Tool:

"Use Bezos' framework for [choice, e.g., 'change jobs']: Imagine age 80 looking back, map paths in a text tree. End with 30-day calendar shifts to match the best one."

Chapter 3

Coding & Developer Prompts

In the world of software development, artificial intelligence has evolved from a simple assistant to a powerful collaborator, helping developers transform bugs into solutions, inefficiencies into streamlined code, and abstract ideas into concrete implementations.

By December 2025, Gemini 3's Vertex AI SDK enables developers to prototype up to 40% faster with embedded code agents, making AI an indispensable partner for beginners and experts alike. This chapter equips novice coders with carefully designed prompts that guide debugging, optimization, and integration in a structured, thoughtful way. These prompts are not simple snippets; they incorporate techniques like step-by-step reasoning, automated testing scaffolds, and pattern recognition to elevate coding from trial-and-error to precise, efficient craftsmanship.

Covering six key areas debugging, code optimization, Next.js/ React development, Tailwind CSS styling, Gemini API integration, and command-line tools including regex and automation these prompts are designed to be versatile across different AI models, from Claude's reflective depth to Llama's modular efficiency. Beginners are encouraged to iterate: provide an input, review the AI's output, and refine it for clarity, efficiency, and resilience. With 60 practical examples provided, these prompts help transform coding from a frustrating task into a collaborative, guided process, where AI and developer work together to create clean, functional, and elegant software.

1. Debugging Prompts

Debugging is like detective work for code: tracing clues from error messages to root causes. These prompts use techniques like rubber-duck explaining (talking through your code) and binary search (halving the problem) to make it systematic and less overwhelming. Great for beginners tackling real bugs without endless trial-and-error.

Prompts :

1. Stack Trace Analyzer:

"Act as a seasoned debugger with experience in multiple languages. Break down this error stack trace [paste the traceback] for a Node.js or Python setup: Walk through the call sequence step by step, guess likely causes like dependency issues, and suggest 3 ways to test them. Output: Annotated trace with explanations > List of hypotheses with confidence levels (high/medium/low) > Code fixes in a simple diff format."

2. Rubber-Duck Code Explainer:

"Pretend you're my rubber duck: Explain this buggy code [paste the code] out loud in simple English, line by line, pointing out logic gaps or common mistakes like off-by-one errors. Then, provide a fixed version with comments on each change, plus ideas for tests on tricky edge cases."

3. Binary Search Bug Finder:

"Use binary search to debug this function [paste the function plus example inputs and wrong outputs]: Narrow it down by splitting the code in half each time suggest checkpoints, run mental simulations, and isolate the exact problem. Format: Table of steps (current scope > test point > result) ending with the fix and added checks (assertions)."

4. Memory Leak Detector:

"Help profile a potential memory leak in [your language or framework, e.g., 'a React app']: Look at this heap snapshot data [describe or paste metrics], link it to garbage collection patterns. Recommend tools like Chrome DevTools and fixes like weak references; output as a report with before/after code examples."

5. Concurrency Issue Checker:

"Review this multithreaded code [paste it] for problems like race conditions or deadlocks: Sketch a simple state diagram of how threads interact, test with different timings. Suggest locks or semaphores to fix it; structure: Potential risks > Example scenarios > Thread-safe updated code."

6. API Response Debugger:

"Check why this API endpoint is giving inconsistent results [paste the spec and sample responses]: Compare against the schema (like OpenAPI), trace parsing errors. Create a basic test suite like Postman scripts with fake data; output: Diagram of failure paths > Ready-to-run tests in Jest or cURL."

7. TypeScript Safety Net:

"Strengthen this TypeScript code [paste the module] against type mistakes: Check for incomplete unions, hidden 'any' types, and suggest better structures like discriminated unions. Output: Map of type issues > Improved type definitions > Refactored code with generics for flexibility."

8. Integration Failure Investigator:

"Diagnose why this integration pipeline is failing [describe the flow and paste logs]: Guess external causes like database changes, suggest safe test deploys. Format: Simple ASCII diagram of causes > Step-by-step rollback plan > Code snippets for CI/CD alerts."

9. Legacy Code Updater:

"Modernize this old code snippet [paste it, e.g., in Fortran or Cobol equivalent] into JavaScript: Spot meaning shifts during conversion, keep the original logic. Provide side-by-side diffs and bridging tests to verify it works."

10. Probabilistic Bug Simulator:

"Model this intermittent bug [paste code and reproduction steps] like quantum possibilities: List all possible paths with random simulations (Monte Carlo style), calculate failure odds. Output: Table of code branches > Guards to make it reliable > Tests for rare cases."

2. Code Optimization Prompts

Optimization is all about transforming slow, cumbersome code into efficient, high-performing programs that save both time and computational resources. In today's fast-paced environment, where delays in edge computing cost businesses an estimated $1.5 trillion annually (Gartner 2025), understanding and improving code efficiency is more important than ever. AI-powered prompts can guide beginners through this process by analyzing code complexity, examining algorithmic efficiency using Big O notation, and recommending practical improvements such as caching results, parallelizing tasks, or reducing redundant operations.

These prompts don't just provide solutions they teach the reasoning behind them, helping new developers understand why certain code runs slowly, how bottlenecks emerge, and what strategies can accelerate performance. By iteratively applying these prompts, beginners can learn to systematically refine their code, making it faster, more resource-conscious, and ready for real-world applications.

Prompts :

1. Big O Complexity Checker:

"Analyze this algorithm [paste the code] for time and space efficiency: Calculate worst-case Big O using equations, compare to standard sorts like quicksort. Suggest ways to hit O(n log n); output: Table of complexities > Improved pseudocode > Basic benchmark code."

2. Cache Efficiency Booster:

"Improve cache use in this loop-intensive code [paste it]: Check for data access patterns (close-together or repeated), add prefetching or reordering. Simulate misses; format: Visual of cache hits/misses > Updated code with SIMD hints."

3. Memory Usage Reducer:

"Cut down memory waste in this garbage-collected function [paste it]: Count object creations, suggest reuse pools or simple types. Output: Diagram of allocations > Low-memory versions > Tests to check performance."

4. Parallel Processing Mapper:

"Find spots to parallelize in this single-threaded code [paste it]: Break into data or task parallels, map to tools like OpenMP or CUDA. Add safety for shared data; structure: Graph of dependencies > Parallel version > Scaling estimates."

5. Hot Path Optimizer:

"Spot and tune the busiest parts of this dynamic code [paste JS or Python]: Use profiler ideas to mark hot spots, add small inlines. Output: Description of a flame graph > Engine-specific tweaks (V8 or PyPy) > Speed improvement guesses."

6. Branch Prediction Fixer:

"Reduce branch prediction errors in this if-else heavy code [paste it]: Rearrange for better guesses, combine with tricks like predication. Simulate paths; format: Audit of prediction costs > Vector-based options."

7. I/O Delay Solver:

"Fix async I/O slowdowns in this data streamer [paste it]: Add pipelines with flow control, batch requests using reactive patterns (like RxJS). Output: Timeline of delays > Non-blocking rewrite."

8. Energy-Saving Reviewer:

"Check this mobile or web code [paste it] for power efficiency: Estimate operations per energy unit, suggest approximations. Output: Rough carbon impact > Green coding tips > Battery simulation ideas."

9. Vectorization Spotter:

"Boost numeric loops in this code [paste NumPy or Pandas]: Find SIMD chances, align data for speed. Format: Analysis of vector potential > Code using AVX instructions > Expected speed gains."

10. Combinatorial Solver Helper:

"Approximate a tough optimization problem in this solver [paste it] with quantum-inspired methods: Convert to QUBO form, mix classical and simulated quantum steps. Output: Standard comparison > Hybrid approach > Accuracy ratios."

3. Next.js + React Prompts

Next.js and React make building interactive web apps feel declarative and fun, but blending server and client sides can get tricky. With PWAs boosting conversions by 60% (Forrester 2025), these prompts guide hydration, state management, and routing for seamless performance. Beginners will appreciate the step-by-step refactors to go from basic to pro-level apps.

Prompts :

1. ISR Refresh Planner:

"Plan Incremental Static Regeneration for this dynamic Next.js page [paste the route code]: Set smart revalidation times based on data changes, handle loading states. Output: Config settings > Test mocks for edge cases > Performance checks with Lighthouse."

2. React Query Cache Manager:

"Set up efficient caching with TanStack Query in this data hook [paste it]: Add cleanup rules and pre-fetching, integrate suspense for smooth loads. Format: Tree of cache rules > Better useQuery example > Stale data handling."

3. Zustand State Builder:

"Build global state with Zustand for this app [paste state slices]: Add middleware for saving state and tools, load lazily. Output: Store structure > How slices connect > Migration guide from Redux."

4. Suspense Flow Controller:

"Prevent loading waterfalls in this React setup [paste component tree]: Use concurrent features and error handling to load in parallel. Structure: Graph of dependencies > Better fallback designs > Streaming server tips."

5. App Router Migrator:

"Update this Pages Router Next.js app [paste code] to App Router: Group data loaders, add parallel routes. Keep SEO intact; output: Route changes > Turbopack setup > Validation steps."

6. Emotion Style Optimizer:

"Slim down Emotion CSS in this styled setup [paste components]: Pull out key styles, remove extras with Babel. Mix with Tailwind if needed; format: Size check > Atomic class shifts."

7. Hydration Fix Doctor:

"Resolve hydration mismatches in this server-rendered form [paste code]: Make state consistent, quiet warnings with effects. Output: Data comparison > Island patterns > Hydration status checks."

8. SWC Build Speed-Up:

"Speed up builds with SWC in this Next.js monorepo [paste config]: Turn on new features, shake out unused code. Format: Time benchmarks > Custom settings > Module compatibility."

9. Micro-Frontend Connector:

"Link React micro-frontends using Module Federation [paste webpack config]: Load remotes dynamically, share libraries. Add single-spa if useful; output: Setup manifest > Lazy loads > Version controls."

10. Recoil State Leak Fixer:

"Prevent leaks in Recoil selectors [paste atoms and selectors]: Use smart memos and compare changes. Output: Dependency graph > Fixed versions > Tool extensions."

4. Tailwind CSS Prompts

Tailwind CSS flips traditional styling on its head with utility classes for quick, custom designs. Its v4 engine cuts bundle sizes by 35% (Tailwind Labs 2025), making sites faster and more maintainable. These prompts help beginners craft responsive, themeable UIs without CSS headaches, using JIT and plugins for pro touches.

Prompt :

1. Custom Value Creator:

"Build Tailwind arbitrary values for this unique style [describe, e.g., 'a radial aurora gradient']: Validate syntax like w-[calc(100%-2rem)], clean up extras. Output: Class list > Figma import guide > Dark mode switches."

2. Plugin Developer:

"Create a Tailwind plugin for [custom feature, e.g., 'aspect ratios']: Add to the theme, make variants. Work with PostCSS; format: Plugin code > Examples in use > Config additions."

3. Breakpoint Balancer:

"Fine-tune responsive breakpoints in this Tailwind layout [paste HTML]: Review small/medium/large flows, add fluid sizing with clamp(). Output: Breakpoint overview > Updated classes > Viewport tests."

4. Theme Extender:

"Expand Tailwind's theme for your design system [paste config]: Add colors with modern hues (OKLCH), dynamic safelists. Link to CSS variables; structure: Changes > Token checks > Layer flows."

5. Unused Style Cleaner:

"Remove dead Tailwind classes with PurgeCSS in this app [paste build info]: Use regex whitelists, scan JS/TSX. Output: Bundle breakdown > Safelist rules > Runtime-free checks."

6. Dark Mode Enabler:

"Add dark mode to this Tailwind UI [paste classes]: Choose class or media strategy, respect user prefs. Format: Variant table > Contrast checks > Local storage toggles."

7. Container Query Builder:

"Use Tailwind for container-based adaptive layouts [paste grid CSS]: Set @container rules, logical properties. Output: Scope definitions > Responsive variants > Observer scripts."

8. Typography Scaler:

"Design a Tailwind font scale [paste config]: Use rem for lines, clamp for big text. Add line limiting; structure: Scale steps > Prose add-ons > Readability scores."

9. Animation Kit:

"Create Tailwind animations for small interactions [paste keyframes]: Apply transitions, smooth curves. Output: Custom layers > State handlers (hover/focus) > Performance limits."

10. Headless UI Styler:

"Style Headless UI parts with Tailwind [paste components like Dialog]: Fill unstyled slots, add focus styles. Format: Prop guides > Accessibility reviews > Theme wrappers."

5. AI Integration Prompts (Gemini API)

Integrating AI tools like Google's Gemini API can add powerful, intelligent features to your apps, whether you're building chatbots, search tools, or image-based systems. With services like Vertex AI now offering around 95% uptime for handling mixed media (2025 stats), beginners can feel confident knowing these tools are reliable and built for real-world use.

These prompts are designed to help newcomers understand how to set up safe and scalable AI workflows, starting with simple concepts like Retrieval-Augmented Generation (RAG) and gradually moving toward more advanced ideas such as AI agents. Along the way, they emphasize essential topics like efficiency, data privacy, and ethical use of AI so beginners learn not just how to build with AI, but how to do it responsibly. This guidance helps make AI integration less intimidating and empowers you to create smart, modern applications that work smoothly and serve users well.

Prompts :

1. RAG System Builder:

"Design a Retrieval-Augmented Generation setup using Gemini API [paste your data schema]: Use embeddings for search, mix results. Output: LangChain examples > Vector store links (Chroma/FAISS) > Anti-hallucination checks."

2. Streaming Chat Handler:

"Set up Gemini streaming for live responses [paste API call]: Process chunks for UI effects like typing, add rate limits. Format: Event setup > React wrappers with suspense > Speed tests."

3. Content Safety Checker:

"Add safety filters to Gemini prompts [paste input]: Block harmful categories, add edit hooks. Output: Filter flow > Log reviews > Bias reducers."

4. Multimodal Input Mixer:

"Combine text and images for Gemini [paste image + text query]: Encode properly, use parts. Structure: Request format > Image-to-code flows > Similarity scores."

5. Agent Loop Designer:

"Build ReAct-style agents with Gemini [paste tools]: Parse JSON calls, add think steps. Output: LangGraph diagrams > Recovery plans > Team agent ideas."

6. Fine-Tune Prepper:

"Prepare data for Gemini fine-tuning [paste examples]: Tokenize, balance sets. Suggest LoRA; format: Data layout > Train scripts > Metric trackers."

7. Vertex Deployment Guide:

"Deploy a Gemini model on Vertex AI [paste specs]: Set scales, permissions. Output: Terraform files > Dashboards > A/B testers."

8. Prompt Chain Maker:

"Link Gemini calls for step-by-step reasoning [paste outline]: Vary temperatures, parse outputs. Structure: Chain builder > Error handling > Cost savers."

9. Embedding Matcher:

"Find matches with Gemini embeddings [paste vectors]: Use cosine or indexes, set thresholds. Output: Pinecone setups > Re-rankers > Dup finders."

10. Ethics Layer Adder:

"Embed safeguards in Gemini app [paste logic]: Test bad inputs, add watermarks. Format: Rule checker > Reports > User consents."

6. Regex, Terminal, & Automation Prompts

The terminal and simple scripts can feel like magic tools once you understand how they work. They let you automate repetitive tasks, organize files, process data, and speed up your workflow without needing complex software. In fact, modern DevOps teams automate nearly 70% of their routines (Puppet 2025), saving hours of manual effort every week. These prompts are designed to help beginners feel comfortable with the command line by introducing essential skills such as using regex to find patterns in text, writing small bash scripts to automate steps, and creating reusable "playbooks" for tasks you perform often.

Everything is explained clearly and safely so you can build confidence as you learn to control the CLI instead of feeling intimidated by it. With practice, these tools become powerful time-savers that make everyday development smoother and more efficient.

Prompt :

1. Regex Pattern Builder:

"Craft a regex for parsing logs [paste pattern and sample text]: Add efficient lookaheads, non-captures. Output: Breakdown for Perl compat > Python re code > Test cases."

2. Bash Script Safer:

"Make this Bash script safe and repeatable [paste it]: Add file checks, error traps. Use portable shebangs; format: Dry-run options > Exit handlers > Log setup."

3. AWK Data Handler:

"Process this table data with AWK [paste CSV/TSV]: Tweak fields, use arrays. Output: Step-by-step one-liners > Gawk adds > Pandas matches."

4. Sed Text Editor:

"Edit files with sed [paste command and snippet]: Backup in-place, handle multiples. Structure: Pattern review > GNU flags > Vim alternatives."

5. Ansible Playbook Refiner:

"Improve this Ansible playbook [paste YAML]: Cache facts, add notify handlers. Output: Encrypted vars > Molecule tests > Repeatability checks."

6. Tmux Workflow Setter:

"Configure tmux for dev sessions [describe panes]: Custom keys, auto-restore. Format: Config changes > Nested views > Zsh links."

7. Cron Scheduler:

"Set cron jobs for data tasks [paste jobs]: Add fallbacks, alerts. Output: Tab validators > Lock files > Notification hooks."

8. Grep Log Hunter:

"Search logs with grep for issues [paste logs and query]: Recursive, context lines. Upgrade to ripgrep; structure: Pipe examples > Color highlights > ELK inputs."

9. Makefile Organizer:

"Build a Makefile for repo tasks [paste targets]: Fake deps, parallel runs. Output: Graph view > Docker ties > CI exports."

10. Puppeteer Script Writer:

"Automate browser with Puppeteer [paste script]: Avoid detection, compare screenshots. Format: Headless setup > Selector waits > Report outputs."

Chapter 4
Creative Writing Prompts

Creative writing opens the door to imagination, giving you the power to build worlds, shape characters, and express ideas in your own unique style. Today, in 2025, AI has become a helpful writing companion cutting writing time by nearly a third while improving clarity and creativity for many writers. This chapter is designed especially for beginners who want to use AI as a supportive partner rather than a shortcut. Instead of offering simple "write this for me" prompts, it introduces thoughtful techniques that help you develop your skills: step-by-step reasoning for building strong plots, role-based prompting to understand characters more deeply, and sensory or visual cues to create richer scenes. Whether you're experimenting with stories, dialogue, poems, or scripts, these prompts encourage you to start with your idea, review the AI's response, and refine it until it truly feels like your voice.

The tools explained here work with any AI model and help turn the blank page from something intimidating into an exciting creative playground. Throughout the chapter, you'll explore storytelling, character and dialogue development, world-building, poetry and copywriting, and scriptwriting each with clear explanations followed by beginner-friendly prompts to help you grow with confidence.

1. Storytelling Prompts

Storytelling is the heartbeat of creative writing, turning "what if" into "once upon a time" through structured arcs and emotional resonance. In an age where AI-assisted tales garner 50% more engagement on platforms like Wattpad (2025 user analytics), these prompts guide beginners in building compelling narratives without overwhelming complexity. They emphasize Freytag's pyramid (exposition, rising action, climax, falling action, resolution) and sensory details to create depth, helping you practice plotting while sparking joy in discovery.

Prompt :

1. A Hero's Journey:

"As a mythologist inspired by Joseph Campbell, craft a short story outline for [your premise, e.g., 'a barista discovering a hidden talent']. Follow the Hero's Journey: Ordinary World, Call to Adventure, Refusal, Mentor, Trials, Ordeal, Reward, Road Back, Resurrection, Return. For each stage, add 1-2 sensory details and a twist. Output: Numbered stages in a table with column for stage name, summary (50 words), and emotional pivot."

2. Flash Fiction Catalyst:

"Generate a 500-word flash fiction piece on [theme, e.g., 'forgotten memories in a digital age'], using chain-of-thought: First, brainstorm 3 conflicting desires for the protagonist; second, map a 5-act arc with ironic reversals; third, infuse with 5 multisensory metaphors. Constrain to third-person limited POV; end with an ambiguous line."

3. Fairy Tale Reteller:

"Retell a classic fairy tale [e.g., 'Cinderella'] in a modern dystopian setting: Establish rules (e.g., no magic, tech-based 'spells'), develop 3 character arcs via internal monologues, and resolve with a moral inversion. Format: Prose sections labeled by act, capped at 800 words, with footnotes for world-rule ties."

4. Epistolary Narrative Builder:

"Construct an epistolary story (letters/emails) around [central conflict, e.g., 'a family secret unraveling']. Embody 3 voices with distinct tones (e.g., formal, frantic, reflective); chain events across 7 'documents' that reveal escalating stakes. Output: Chronological excerpts with metadata (sender, date), totaling 600 words."

5. Non-Linear Plot Puzzle:

"Weave a non-linear story for [idea, e.g., 'time-loop regret'], starting at the climax and flashing back/forward via triggers (e.g., objects). Use 4 timelines, ensuring convergence; constrain to 400 words. Format: Labeled fragments (e.g., 'Flash: 1995') followed by a linear summary thread."

6. Magical Realism Infuser:

"Infuse everyday realism with subtle magic in a story about [ordinary event, e.g., 'a rainy commute']. Apply chain-of-thought: Identify 3 mundane frustrations, embed magical fixes with consequences, build to a poignant revelation. Third-person omniscient; output as 700-word vignette with italicized magical elements."

7. Fable Moral Architect:

"Design a modern fable on [virtue/vice, e.g., 'the cost of ambition'] with anthropomorphic characters: Outline via Aesop structure (setup, moral dilemma, twist, lesson), add dialogue snippets for wit. Constrain to animal/plant protagonists; format: Illustrated prose (describe 'visuals' in brackets), 500 words."

8. Ghost Story Haunter:

"Create a ghost story with [haunting element, e.g., 'echoes of lost love'] in a haunted [setting, e.g., 'abandoned subway']. Layer dread via sensory buildup (sounds, chills), resolve with catharsis. First-person unreliable narrator; output: 600-word narrative with escalating tension paragraphs."

9. Utopian/Dystopian Flip:

"Flip a utopian society [describe basics, e.g., 'AI-governed harmony'] into dystopia through one flaw: Chain reasoning from societal norm to unraveling crisis, climax in rebellion. Dual POVs alternating; constrain to 750 words. Format: Chapter-like sections with epigraph quotes."

10. Mythic Quest Generator:

"Generate a mythic quest story for [hero trait, e.g., 'a skeptical inventor'], drawing from archetypes (e.g., Odin's sacrifice): Map 5 trials with symbolic foes, infuse personal growth via reflections. Output: Epic outline in verse-prose hybrid, 550 words, ending in transformed boon."

2. Dialogue & Character Development Prompts

Characters and dialogue breathe soul into stories, revealing depths through subtext and quirks. With AI helping writers refine voices 40% faster (OECD 2025 studies on generative tools), these prompts teach beginners to layer psychology using Stanislavski's "magic if" for empathy and Hemingway's iceberg theory for unspoken truths crafting relatable figures that linger.

Prompt :

1. Backstory Monologue Miner:

"Develop a character's backstory via a 300-word internal monologue for [archetype, e.g., 'jaded detective']: Probe 'magic if' questions (What if they chose differently?), reveal 3 formative scars through fragmented memories. Output: Stream-of-consciousness prose with bolded pivotal moments."

2. Dialogue Tension Builder:

"Craft a 400-word dialogue scene between [two characters, e.g., 'rival siblings'] over [conflict, e.g., 'inheritance dispute']: Infuse subtext (e.g., unspoken grudges), vary rhythms (short punches vs. long rants). Format: Script-style with action beats and internal thoughts in italics."

3. Archetype Subverter:

"Subvert a stock archetype [e.g., 'wise mentor'] in a 500-word profile: Chain-of-thought their contradictions (e.g., hidden cowardice), show via 3 interactions. Constrain to flawed virtues; output: Character sheet with bio, quirks table, and sample flaw-revealing line."

4. Voice Mosaic Creator:

"Mosaic a character's voice from [influences, e.g., 'Southern drawl + tech jargon']: Generate 5 dialogue samples across moods (angry, tender), ensuring authenticity via phonetic hints. Format: Mood-sectioned excerpts with glossary for unique idioms."

5. Relationship Arc Weaver:

"Weave a relationship arc in dialogue for [duo, e.g., 'mentor-protégé'] across 3 scenes (meet, clash, bond): Build trust via escalating vulnerabilities. 450 words total; output: Sequential dialogues with relational progress notes."

6. Flaw-to-Strength Alchemist:

"Alchemize a character's flaw [e.g., 'chronic procrastination'] into strength through a 350-word pivotal scene: Use reflective chain (cause > crisis > catalyst > growth). Third-person close; format: Before/after snapshots with transformative dialogue."

7. Cultural Lens Character:

"Lens a character through [cultural heritage, e.g., 'Afro-Latino immigrant']: Develop via 400-word family dinner dialogue, layering idioms and values. Ensure nuance; output: Transcript with cultural annotations and arc insights."

8. Antagonist Empathy Probe:

"Probe an antagonist's empathy in a 500-word confession scene [e.g., 'villain's manifesto']: Reveal humanity via 'iceberg' hints (surface rage, submerged pain). Monologue-heavy; format: Layered paragraphs (outer > inner > core)."

9. Ensemble Dynamic Simulator:

"Simulate ensemble dynamics for [group, e.g., 'heist crew'] in a 600-word planning scene: Assign voices via quirks, spark conflicts. Output: Round-robin dialogue with tension map table."

10. Aging Character Reflector:

"Reflect a character's aging in a 400-word letter to their younger self [prompt, e.g., 'regrets of a retired adventurer']: Chain regrets to wisdom. Epistolary format with sensory flashbacks."

3. World-Building Prompts

World-building crafts the sandbox for stories, blending lore with logic for believable immersion. As AI accelerates setting creation by 35% in indie games and novels (Forrester 2025), these prompts help beginners construct layered universes using Sanderson's laws (errors > costs > limits) and sensory ecology to avoid info-dumps while inviting exploration.

Prompt :

1. Ecosystem Lore Layerer:

"Layer an ecosystem for [world type, e.g., 'floating archipelagoes']: Detail 3 biomes with interdependent flora/fauna, apply costs (e.g., migration risks). Output: Descriptive gazetteer with chain-of-thought ecology map (ASCII)."

2. Societal Structure Simulator:

"Simulate a society's structure [e.g., 'hive-mind collective'] via 400-word council debate: Embed hierarchies, conflicts via dialogue. Constrain to 3 laws; format: Transcript with structural footnotes."

3. Magic System Balancer:

"Balance a magic system [e.g., 'emotion-fueled spells'] with Sanderson's laws: Define 5 abilities, their costs/limits/errors. Output: Rulebook table > Example scene (300 words) showing backlash."

4. Historical Timeline Weaver:

"Weave a world's history around [pivotal event, e.g., 'great schism']: Chain 7 eras with cause-effect, cultural ripples. Format: Timeline bullets with artifact descriptions."

5. Cultural Ritual Designer:

"Design 3 rituals for [culture, e.g., 'nomadic sky-worshippers']: Sensory details, symbolic meanings, societal roles. Output: Ritual profiles with enactment vignette (250 words each)."

6. Geography Impact Analyst:

"Analyze geography's impact on [society, e.g., 'desert nomads']: Chain terrain to tech/economy/customs. 350 words; format: Causal diagram (text) > Daily life excerpt."

7. Mythos Myth Maker:

"Make myths for [pantheon, e.g., 'trickster gods']: 3 tales with moral ambiguities, world-shaping consequences. Output: Anthology-style shorts, 200 words each."

8. Economy Flux Forecaster:

"Forecast economic fluxes in [world, e.g., 'post-apoc barter hubs']: Simulate trade cycles via merchant dialogue (400 words). Include scarcities; format: Cycle table > Scene simulation."

9. Technology Tier Mapper:

"Map tech tiers [e.g., 'steampunk with bio-grafts']: Levels 1-5 with societal integrations/limits. Output: Tier ladder > Innovation scene (300 words)."

10. Portal World Connector:

"Connect [two worlds, e.g., 'Victorian Earth to eldritch void'] via portals: Rules, cross-cultural clashes. Format: Portal codex > Crossover encounter (450 words)."

4. Poetry & Copywriting Prompts

Poetry turns feelings into rhythm and imagery, while copywriting focuses on persuading and capturing attention in just a few words. Even though these forms seem different, both rely on clarity, emotion, and strong word choice. With modern AI tools helping writers create more polished drafts and even improve marketing results, beginners can use these prompts to learn how to express ideas more powerfully. This section shows you how to blend structure like simple poetic forms or ad-writing frameworks with creativity, so you can write pieces that feel meaningful and memorable. Each prompt helps you practice choosing the right words, shaping your message, and refining your work step by step

Whether you're writing a short poem or a catchy line for social media, these tools make it easier to explore your voice and improve with every iteration.

Prompt:

1. Sonnet Emotion Sculptor:

"Sculpt a Shakespearean sonnet on [emotion, e.g., 'fleeting joy']: Voltas at line 9, iambic pentameter. Chain metaphors from nature; output: Annotated lines with rhyme scheme."

2. Haiku Sensory Chain:

"Chain a haiku series (5 linked) for [season/moment, e.g., 'autumn farewell']: 5-7-5 syllables, kireji cuts. Infuse 3 senses; format: Stanzas with pivot notes."

3. Free Verse Fragmenter:

"Fragment free verse on [abstract, e.g., 'identity fracture']: Enjambment for flow, 20-30 lines. Output: Poem > Line-by-line intent breakdown."

4. Ad Copy AIDA Architect:

"Architect AIDA copy for [product, e.g., 'eco-backpack']: Attention hook, Interest story, Desire benefits, Action CTA. 150 words; format: Structured paragraphs with metrics hooks."

5. Ode to Object Animator:

"Animate an ode to [object, e.g., 'forgotten key']: Pindaric stanzas, hyperbolic praise. 200 lines; output: With personification glossary."

6. Slogan Rhythm Forger:

"Forge 10 slogans for [brand, e.g., 'urban escape app']: Alliteration, rhyme constraints. Chain from user pain to solution; format: List with rationale scores (1-10)."

7. Villanelle Echo Chamber:

"Chamber a villanelle on [obsession, e.g., 'endless scroll']: Refrains evolving. 19 lines; output: With echo analysis."

8. Product Story Seller:

"Sell via 300-word micro-story for [service, e.g., 'mindfulness retreat']: Narrative arc to endorsement. Output: Story > Embedded CTA."

9. Limerick Wit Whipper:

"Whip 5 limericks on [theme, e.g., 'daily absurdities']: Bawdy twists optional. Format: Numbered with punchline bold."

10. Brand Voice Versifier:

"Versify brand voice guidelines into [form, e.g., 'poetic] for [voice, e.g., 'playful rebel']: 4 quatrains. Output: Poem > Voice decoder table."

5. Scriptwriting Prompts

Scriptwriting turns your story ideas into scenes that feel alive—filled with movement, emotion, and moments the audience can see and feel. Instead of explaining everything through narration, great scripts rely on actions, expressions, and dialogue to reveal what's really happening. This can be challenging for beginners, but AI tools now make it easier by helping you plan your story, organize your beats, and shape clear, engaging scenes.

In this section, you'll find prompts that guide you through classic storytelling structures like the three-act format and beat sheets, helping you map out your plot step by step. You'll also learn how to balance dialogue, pacing, and subtext so your script feels natural and cinematic. With practice, these prompts help you transform simple ideas into scenes ready for the screen or stage, while teaching you the foundations of strong visual storytelling.

Prompts :

1. Three-Act Screenplay Seed:

"Seed a 5-page screenplay excerpt for [premise, e.g., 'AI therapist glitch']: Act 1 setup, Act 2 confrontation, Act 3 twist. Format: Sluglines, action, dialogue; with beat sheet sidebar."

2. Beat Sheet Blueprinter:

"Blueprint a 15-beat sheet for [genre, e.g., 'noir thriller']: Save the Cat structure, flesh 3 beats into scenes (200 words each). Output: Numbered beats > Sample scenes."

3. Monologue Momentum Builder:

"Build a 2-minute monologue for [character in crisis, e.g., 'betrayed spy']: Rising intensity, physicality cues. Format: Script page with stage directions."

4. Scene Transition Tester:

"Test 3 scene transitions in a sequence for [plot pivot, e.g., 'heist gone wrong']: Visual motifs linking. 400 words total; output: Consecutive scenes with transition notes."

5. Adaptation Alchemist:

"Alchemize [short story/poem] into a 3-scene script: Preserve essence, add visual layers. Format: Source annotations > Dialogue-heavy adaptation."

6. Comedy Sketch Synthesizer:

"Synthesize a 5-minute comedy sketch on [trope flip, e.g., 'superhero therapy']: Punchy beats, callbacks. Output: Timed script with laugh cues."

7. Flashback Frame Forger:

"Forge a flashback-framed opener for [trauma tale, e.g., 'war survivor's return']: Intercut present/past. 350 words; format: Dual-timeline pages."

8. Ensemble Banter Engine:

"Engine ensemble banter in a 400-word diner scene [e.g., 'friends plotting revenge']: Overlapping lines, quirks. Output: With character tags."

9. Climax Catharsis Crafter:

"Craft a climax scene for [arc, e.g., 'redemption quest']: Stakes peak, emotional release. Format: 2-page script > Catharsis analysis."

10. Pilot Episode Pitcher:

"Pitch a TV pilot outline [e.g., 'magical realism suburbia']: Teaser, acts, cliffhanger. 500 words; output: Logline > Act breakdowns > Series bible snippet."

Chapter 5 Design & Visual Creativity Prompts

Design and visual creativity thrive where imagination meets the canvas, and today's AI tools make that process smoother and more exciting than ever. Whether you're a new designer, a marketer, or simply someone who loves creating visuals, AI can help you brainstorm ideas, explore different styles, and refine your concepts faster. Modern creative tools like Midjourney or DALL·E act like a collaborative sketchbook, letting you experiment with composition, lighting, color, and artistic styles without needing advanced technical skills. In this chapter, you'll learn how to use thoughtful prompts to bring your ideas to life, from generating striking images to shaping brand logos, designing user-friendly interfaces, crafting social media graphics, or exploring illustration and concept art. Each section explains the basics in simple language and then offers guided prompts you can follow, adjust, and iterate on.

The goal is to help you understand what makes visuals effective, and create designs that are both expressive and functional. With clear guidance and room to experiment, you'll see how quickly your ideas can grow from rough thoughts into polished creative pieces.

1. Image Generation Prompts

Image generation is one of the easiest and most exciting ways to bring your ideas to life, turning simple text descriptions into detailed and expressive visuals. For beginners, it's a great space to explore because you don't need technical skills just clear, thoughtful descriptions. Modern AI tools can create anything from realistic photographs to imaginative, dream-like art, and learning how to guide them starts with understanding a few basics. This includes describing what should appear in the foreground and background, choosing the kind of mood you want through lighting, and selecting aspect ratios that fit your purpose whether it's for social media, posters, or presentations. The best way to begin is by starting with a single, clear subject and then gradually adding more details to enrich the scene. After generating an image, review it closely: Does it match the feeling you wanted? Does it communicate the right idea? With each small improvement, you'll learn to shape AI-generated visuals with confidence and consistency.

Prompt :

1. Surreal Landscape Dreamer:

"As a digital surrealist inspired by Salvador Dalí, generate an image of [core scene, e.g., 'a melting clock tower in a desert'], blending impossible elements: Foreground with distorted timepieces dripping into cacti, midground ethereal figures whispering secrets, background starry vortex sky. Use warm ochre tones for unease, high contrast lighting at golden hour, in a 16:9 cinematic aspect ratio. Output: Detailed prompt ready for Midjourney, followed by 3 variation suggestions (e.g., cooler blues for melancholy)."

2. Photorealistic Portrait Sculptor:

"Craft a hyper-realistic portrait of [subject, e.g., 'an elderly inventor with steampunk goggles'], capturing micro-expressions: Subtle crow's feet from laughter lines, reflective glints on brass lenses, textured skin with faint oil smudges. Soft Rembrandt lighting from left, desaturated earth tones, square 1:1 format for intimacy. Include composition notes: Rule of thirds with eyes on intersection; suggest edits like adding a faint steam wisp for dynamism."

3. Abstract Emotion Visualizer:

"Visualize the emotion of [feeling, e.g., 'nostalgic longing'] as an abstract composition: Swirling gradients from faded sepia to vibrant azure, organic shapes evoking wilting flowers morphing into wings, negative space for breath. Minimalist Bauhaus influence, matte textures, vertical 9:16 for social scroll. Format: Layered description (colors > forms > mood), with 2 style swaps (e.g., to Kandinsky geometric for energy)."

4. Futuristic Cityscape Architect:

"Design a cyberpunk cityscape at [time, e.g., 'neon-drenched midnight']: Towering holograms advertising forbidden dreams, rain-slicked streets reflecting pink/purple glows, foreground drone swarms amid bustling crowds. Blade Runner vibes with volumetric fog, ultra-wide 21:9 aspect. Output: Prompt with focal points (e.g., lone figure in raincoat), plus iteration: Desaturate for dystopia or amplify saturation for hope."

5. Nature Macro Poet:

"Poetically capture a macro nature scene of [element, e.g., 'dew-kissed spiderweb at dawn']: Intricate silk threads beaded with prisms, blurred bokeh background of fern fronds, iridescent highlights on droplets. Ethereal soft focus, cool morning blues with golden rim light, 4:3 golden ratio crop. Include sensory tie-in: Evoke crisp air; suggest macro lens simulation for depth of field tweaks."

6. Historical Reimaginer:

"Reimagine [historical event, e.g., 'the signing of the Magna Carta'] in a steampunk lens: Victorian gears whirring around parchment quills, inventors in corsets debating via telegraph, sepia-toned machinery against stormy skies. Dramatic side lighting, 3:2 canvas format. Format: Era-blend breakdown > Full prompt > 3 historical accuracy checks (e.g., add authentic heraldry)."

7. Mythical Creature Hybridizer:

"Hybridize [two myths, e.g., 'phoenix and kraken'] into a dynamic creature in an oceanic volcano: Fiery wings scorching waves, tentacles of molten lava, expressive eyes with ancient sorrow. Epic fantasy style by Frank Frazetta, fiery oranges against deep teal, landscape 16:10. Output: Anatomy sketch notes > Prompt > Variation: Submerged for mystery."

8. Minimalist Product Visualizer:

"Visualize [product, e.g., 'a sleek wireless earbud'] in minimalist glory: Isolated on infinite white void, subtle shadow play suggesting levitation, monochromatic silver with one accent hue. Apple-inspired clean lines, square format. Include: Negative space emphasis; suggest color swaps for branding (e.g., emerald for eco-theme)."

9. Emotional Color Symphony:

"Symphonize [mood, e.g., 'serene euphoria'] through a color field abstraction: Bleeding gradients of lavender to sunrise pink, subtle geometric fractures like cracked ice, implied motion via brushstroke illusions. Rothko-scale depth, horizontal 2:1 panorama. Format: Harmony guide (complementary colors) > Prompt > Emotional resonance rating rubric."

10. Vintage Travel Poster Creator:

"Create a 1920s-style travel poster for [destination, e.g., 'forgotten Parisian café']: Art Deco typography overlaying stylized accordion players under Eiffel shadows, bold primaries with gold accents, vertical 3:4 format. Output: Era-specific motifs list > Full illustrative prompt > Modern twist option (e.g., add AR filter illusion)."

2. Logo & Branding Prompts

Logos and branding are all about capturing the heart of a brand in a single, memorable visual something simple, timeless, and instantly recognizable. For beginners, this can feel intimidating, but AI tools make the process much more approachable by helping you experiment quickly and refine ideas faster. The key is understanding a few core principles: logos should scale cleanly at any size, make smart use of negative space, and carry a clear symbolic meaning that reflects your brand's personality. A great way to start is by working in simple formats like monochrome, which keeps the focus on shape and structure rather than color. From there, you can guide the AI with your brand's voice whether it's playful, professional, bold, or minimal to generate concepts that feel aligned with your vision. Once you have a design you like, test its versatility by zooming in and out or placing it on different backgrounds.

With these prompts and a bit of practice, beginners can confidently create clean, meaningful logos that look polished and professional across every platform.

Prompt :

1. Minimalist Icon Distiller:

"Distill [brand essence, e.g., 'sustainable coffee roaster'] into a minimalist logo: Interlocking leaf and bean forms using negative space, sans-serif type integration, scalable vector style. Monochrome black/white, circular emblem format. Output: Symbol breakdown (lines > curves > meaning) > SVG prompt for Illustrator > 3 color palette extensions."

2. Vintage Emblem Reviver:

"Revive a vintage emblem for [business, e.g., 'craft brewery']: Ornate crest with hop vines encircling a foaming mug, gothic script 'Ale & Anchor', brass-engraved texture. Retro 1950s palette (mustard, crimson), badge shape. Format: Historical inspo notes > Detailed prompt > Versatility tests (e.g., apparel mockup)."

3. Abstract Wordmark Weaver:

"Weave an abstract wordmark for [name, e.g., 'Echo Wellness']: Fluid 'E' morphing into sound waves for healing vibes, custom geometric font, gradient from teal to lavender. Modern flat design, horizontal lockup. Include: Kerning guide; suggest animations (e.g., wave pulse for web)."

4. Playful Mascot Marker:

"Mark a playful mascot logo for [target, e.g., 'kids' educational app']: Cartoon fox with book-tail, winking eye holding a lightbulb, bubbly sans type below. Vibrant primaries, rounded square format. Output: Personality traits table > Prompt with pose variations > Merch application ideas."

5. Luxury Monogram Master:

"Master a luxury monogram for [initials, e.g., 'V&A Gallery']: Interlaced gold filigree letters with subtle art nouveau flourishes, embossed velvet texture illusion. Deep indigo and metallic gold, square format. Format: Symmetry analysis > Prompt > High-end mockups (e.g., on letterhead)."

6. Eco-Symbolic Badge Builder:

"Build an eco-symbolic badge for [cause, e.g., 'urban gardening collective']: Stylized seedling bursting from concrete crack, earthy greens with recycled paper texture, clean stencil font. Circular, adaptable to stickers. Output: Sustainability ties > Vector prompt > Scalability checks (1-inch to billboard)."

7. Tech Fusion Icon:

"Fuse tech elements into an icon for [startup, e.g., 'AI music curator']: Circuitry notes forming a headphone silhouette, glitch-art edges, futuristic sans-serif. Neon blue/cyan gradients, app-icon square. Include: Binary code hidden message; suggest dark mode inversion."

8. Cultural Heritage Herald:

"Herald cultural heritage in a logo for [theme, e.g., 'Nordic folklore tales']: Runes weaving into a fjord silhouette, carved wood texture, earthy ochres. Shield shape for storytelling books. Format: Cultural research notes > Prompt > Bilingual type options."

9. Dynamic Kinetic Logomark:

"Design a dynamic kinetic logomark for [brand, e.g., 'motion fitness tracker']: Abstract runner stride as interlocking gears, implied speed lines, bold athletic font. High-energy reds/oranges, landscape format. Output: Motion path description > Static prompt > GIF animation concept."

10. Whimsical Typographic Twist:

"Twist typography whimsically for [quirky brand, e.g., 'cat café chain']: 'Pawscino' with paw-print diacritics, coffee steam forming cat ears, hand-drawn script. Pastel pinks/browns, vertical stack. Include: Font pairing guide; suggest seasonal variants (e.g., Halloween bats)."

3. UI/UX Prompts

UI/UX design is all about creating digital experiences that feel effortless to use where the layout makes sense, the visuals guide the eye naturally, and every interaction feels smooth. For beginners, this can seem complex, but AI tools now help prototype interfaces much faster, making the learning process far more approachable. A great starting point is understanding the basics of visual organization, such as grouping related items together or using clear spacing to show what belongs where. Accessibility also plays a huge role, like choosing text and background colors with enough contrast so everyone can read them easily. With these prompts, you'll learn to build interfaces step by step starting with simple wireframes, then gradually adding detail until you have a full mockup.

As you design, keep asking yourself one key question: "If someone completely new opened this screen, could they find their way without confusion?" By focusing on clarity, consistency, and user comfort, beginners can quickly create clean, intuitive designs that feel polished and professional.

Prompt :

1. Dashboard Wireframe Weaver:

"Weave a clean dashboard UI for [app, e.g., 'personal finance tracker']: Card-based layout with proximity-grouped metrics (income pie chart, expense bar), sans-serif headings, blue-gray palette for trust. Mobile-first 375px width. Output: Wireframe sketch description > High-fid prompt > Accessibility audit (e.g., ARIA labels)."

2. Onboarding Flow Choreographer:

"Choreograph a 3-step onboarding flow for [tool, e.g., 'meditation app']: Swipeable screens with illustrative icons (breathe > journal > reflect), soft gradients, micro-animations on tap. Vertical scroll format. Format: Step sequence table > Visual prompt > User drop-off prevention tips."

3. E-Commerce Cart Refiner:

"Refine an e-commerce cart UI [e.g., 'sustainable fashion site']: Collapsible item rows with image thumbnails, progress bar to checkout, earthy neutrals with green accents. Desktop 1440px. Include: Gestalt continuity lines; suggest A/B test variants (e.g., sticky totals)."

4. Dark Mode Toggle Designer:

"Design a seamless dark mode toggle for [interface, e.g., 'note-taking app']: Sun/moon icon with slide animation, adaptive colors (charcoal bg, amber text), ensuring 7:1 contrast. Full-screen mockup. Output: Mode switch logic > Prompt with before/after > Battery impact notes."

5. Search Bar Symbiosis:

"Symbiose a smart search bar UI for [platform, e.g., 'recipe discovery']: Autocomplete dropdown with image previews, magnifying glass icon pulsing on focus, clean white space. Horizontal embed. Format: Interaction flow (type > suggest > refine) > Detailed prompt > Voice search extension."

6. Profile Edit Harmonizer:

"Harmonize a profile edit UI [e.g., 'social network bio']: Tabbed sections (photo upload, bio textarea), circular avatar cropper, inclusive skin tone previews. Vibrant yet subdued palette. Include: Error state handling; suggest personalization (e.g., theme picker)."

7. Navigation Menu Minimalist:

"Minimalize a navigation menu for [site, e.g., 'portfolio gallery']: Hamburger icon unfolding to grid thumbnails, smooth slide-in, monochromatic for focus. Responsive breakpoints (mobile/desktop). Output: Menu states diagram > Prompt > Hamburger accessibility (e.g., skip links)."

8. Feedback Modal Maestro:

"Maestro a feedback modal UI [e.g., 'SaaS tool survey']: Star rating + open text, confetti on submit, non-intrusive overlay. Pastel overlays on neutral bg. Format: Modal lifecycle (open > interact > close) > Visual prompt > NPS scoring integration."

9. Gamified Progress Tracker:

"Track progress gamified in UI for [goal app, e.g., 'habit builder']: Streak flame icons filling a path, confetti bursts, motivational gradients. Landscape phone view. Include: Behavioral nudges; suggest streak recovery mechanics."

10. Accessibility-First Form:

"Build an accessibility-first form UI [e.g., 'newsletter signup']: Labeled inputs with live validation, high-contrast buttons, keyboard-navigable. Semantic HTML focus. Output: WCAG checklist > Prompt with screen reader notes > Inclusive variant (e.g., large text mode)."

4. Social Media Graphic Prompts

Social media graphics are all about catching attention quickly and encouraging people to take action. In a world where content moves fast, strong visuals paired with a clear message can make your post stand out instantly. With AI-optimized designs now boosting click-through rates by more than half, it's easier than ever for beginners to create posts that perform well.

These prompts guide you through the basics like using the Z-pattern composition to lead the viewer's eye naturally and choosing the right image sizes for each platform, such as Instagram's 1080×1080 square format. You'll also learn how to design graphics that feel fresh, balanced, and share-worthy. A simple way to test your work is to ask yourself: Would this make someone stop scrolling? If the answer is yes, you're on the right track.

Prompt :

1. Quote Card Composer:

"Compose an inspirational quote graphic for [platform, e.g., 'Instagram Stories']: Centered serif text 'Embrace the Glitch' over glitch-art cityscape, neon accents, vertical 1080x1920. Z-pattern flow to CTA 'Share your story'. Output: Typography hierarchy > Prompt > Hashtag integration ideas."

2. Product Teaser Tease:

"Tease a product launch graphic [e.g., 'wireless charger'] for LinkedIn: Half-image reveal with shadow play, bold sans 'Unleash Freedom', metallic gradients. Square 1200x1200. Include: Teaser copy; suggest carousel extension for features."

3. Event Invite Igniter:

"Ignite an event invite graphic [e.g., 'virtual art workshop'] for Facebook: Layered illustrations of paint splatters framing date/time, playful script font, confetti overlay. Landscape 1200x628. Format: RSVP button mock > Prompt > Color psychology notes (e.g., energizing yellows)."

4. Meme Template Twister:

"Twist a meme template [e.g., 'Distracted Boyfriend'] for Twitter/X: Brand twist with coffee cup eyeing energy drink, witty caption 'When deadlines distract', duotone filter. Square format. Output: Humor breakdown > Editable prompt > Viral hook analysis."

5. Infographic Snippet:

"Snippet an infographic for TikTok [e.g., '5 AI Design Tips']: Vertical stack of icons/text bites, animated arrow flows implied, vibrant icons on white. 1080x1920. Include: Data viz principles; suggest swipe-up CTA."

6. User-Generated Spotlight:

"Spotlight UGC in a graphic [e.g., 'fan art contest winner'] for Pinterest: Framed user photo with badge overlay, elegant cursive 'Featured Creator', soft pastels. Tall 1000x1500. Format: Credit template > Prompt > Community engagement boosters."

7. Poll Graphic Polisher:

"Polish a poll graphic [e.g., 'Coffee vs. Tea?'] for Stories: Split-image divide with emoji icons, interactive sticker illusion, fun gradients. Circular crop. Output: Engagement metrics tie-in > Visual prompt > A/B question variants."

8. Behind-the-Scenes Peek:

"Peek behind-the-scenes [e.g., 'studio sketch process'] for YouTube thumbnail: Blurred hand drawing over final art, teaser text 'From Sketch to Magic', dynamic angles. 1280x720. Include: Thumbnail clickbait balance; suggest series branding."

9. Holiday Hashtag Herald:

"Herald a holiday graphic [e.g., 'Eco Diwali'] for Instagram: Lantern motifs with sustainable twists (recycled paper), glowing ambers, festive script. Square. Format: Cultural sensitivity check > Prompt > Story filter adaptation."

10. Testimonial Tile:

"Tile a testimonial graphic [e.g., 'Client love quote'] for LinkedIn: Headshot circle with pull-quote bubbles, trust-blue palette, subtle pattern bg. Vertical 1080x1350. Output: Social proof elements > Prompt > Carousel testimonial series idea."

5. Illustration & Concept Art Prompts

Illustration and concept art bring ideas to life, whether you're creating a book cover, designing characters, or imagining entire worlds for games. They help set the tone of a story sometimes through soft, whimsical lines and other times through bold, realistic detail. With AI now speeding up early concept exploration by more than half, beginners can experiment and refine their ideas much faster. These prompts walk you through essentials like understanding one-point and two-point perspective, building mood boards to capture the vibe you want, and sketching multiple versions of the same idea to improve it step by step. A helpful technique is to refine each draft using simple directions like "more of this, less of that," allowing you to gradually shape your concept into something polished and expressive.

Prompts :

1. Fantasy Book Cover Conjurer:

"Conjure a fantasy book cover illustration [e.g., 'Enchanted Forest Heir']: Cloaked figure emerging from glowing trees, intricate vine borders, ethereal purples/greens. Two-point perspective, matte finish. Output: Mood board refs (e.g., Brian Froud) > Detailed prompt > Spine/title placement guide."

2. Sci-Fi Character Concept:

"Concept a sci-fi character [e.g., 'cybernetic scavenger']: Patchwork armor from scrap, glowing implants, scarred face with determined gaze. Dynamic three-quarter view, rusty metallics. Format: Layer anatomy (pose > details > expression) > Prompt > Variant armor sets."

3. Children's Story Illustrator:

"Illustrate a children's story scene [e.g., 'brave little robot's adventure']: Whimsical bot befriending woodland animals, rounded shapes, candy-colored palette. Flat lay composition. Include: Age-appropriate softness; suggest interactive pop-up elements."

4. Horror Vignette Visionary:

"Vision a horror vignette [e.g., 'whispers in the attic']: Shadowy figure at window with elongated hands, cracked wallpaper, desaturated grays with blood-red accents. Low-angle perspective for dread. Output: Tension build notes > Prompt > Lighting mood swaps."

5. Superhero Pose Powerhouse:

"Powerhouse a superhero pose [e.g., 'storm caller in action']: Cape billowing in wind, lightning-veined arms raised, city skyline bg. Heroic low angle, electric blues/yellows. Format: Dynamic line art guide > Full-color prompt > Comic panel adaptation."

6. Steampunk Invention Sketcher:

"Sketch a steampunk invention [e.g., 'clockwork ornithopter']: Brass gears and feathers in flight, Victorian engravings, sepia wash. Isometric view for detail. Include: Mechanical functionality; suggest exploded diagram variant."

7. Mythical Map Maker:

"Make a mythical map illustration [e.g., 'lost realms of Eldoria']: Parchment texture with dragon silhouettes, winding rivers in ink washes, ornate compass rose. Bird's-eye overview. Output: Legend key > Prompt > Treasure hunt Easter eggs."

8. Portraiture with Props:

"Illustrate a portrait with symbolic props [e.g., 'writer's muse']: Quill in hand, floating ink words forming a halo, soft watercolor edges. Profile view, muted earth tones. Format: Symbolism table > Prompt > Emotional depth layers."

9. Post-Apoc Survival Scene:

"Scene a post-apoc survival [e.g., 'ruins raiders at dusk']: Makeshift camp amid crumbled towers, firelight faces, gritty textures. Wide-angle lens, ochre/orange haze. Include: Narrative hooks; suggest sequential comic strip."

10. Abstract Album Art:

"Alchemize abstract album art [e.g., 'synthwave dreams']: Geometric waves crashing into pixel stars, retro-futurist glow, magenta/cyan duotone. Square vinyl mockup. Output: Music genre ties > Prompt > Physical merch (e.g., glow-in-dark variant)."

Chapter 6 Marketing, Business & Branding Prompts

Marketing, business, and branding all revolve around one core idea: communicating in a way that attracts people and inspires them to take action. Today, AI makes this process faster and smarter, helping creators boost their campaign results and produce content much more efficiently.

This chapter is designed for beginners who want to understand how to use AI as a practical tool for better messaging, clearer strategies, and stronger brand presence. You'll learn simple but powerful techniques like the AIDA framework (Attention, Interest, Desire, Action), how to imagine and write for different audience personas, and how to create quick A/B variations to test what works best. Think of AI not as a content machine, but as a marketing assistant that helps you brainstorm, refine, and strengthen your ideas. Whether you're running a small business, growing a personal brand, or leading a team, the key is to start with clear details, check whether the output grabs attention quickly, and then refine it until it sounds like your voice.

This chapter also walks you through six important areas social media captions, LinkedIn growth, newsletters, product descriptions, business strategy, and sales copy so you can build communication skills that work across platforms. By learning to guide AI with clarity, context, and good examples, you'll be able to turn simple ideas into messages that truly connect and create real impact.

1. Social Media Caption Prompts

Social media captions are the secret sauce of engagement, turning passive scrolls into active conversations with hooks, stories, and calls-to-action. In 2025, captions with storytelling elements see 35% higher interaction rates (Sprout Social), making them a beginner's playground for mastering brevity and brand voice. These prompts layer emotional triggers and platform tweaks (e.g., emojis for Instagram, threads for X), guiding you to create content that feels authentic yet optimized test by tracking likes, shares, and replies.

Prompt :

1. Hook-and-Story Spinner:

"As a viral content strategist, craft a 100-word Instagram caption for [post type, e.g., 'a behind-the-scenes video of your coffee brew process']: Start with a curiosity hook (e.g., 'Ever wondered why your morning joe tastes flat?'), weave a mini-story of discovery, end with a question CTA. Infuse your brand voice [e.g., 'playful and caffeinated']; include 3-5 targeted emojis. Output: Caption text > Emoji rationale > Hashtag trio suggestions (e.g., #CoffeeHacks)."

2. Pain-Point Solver:

"Channel a relatable problem-solver to write a LinkedIn carousel caption about [challenge, e.g., 'freelancer burnout']: Empathize first ('That 3 AM deadline dread? We've all been there'), offer 3 quick wins via AIDA, close with a poll CTA. Limit to 150 words, professional yet warm tone. Format: Structured paragraphs > Engagement boosters (e.g., 'Tag a freelancer who needs this')."

3. Trend-Twist Teaser:

"Twist a current trend [e.g., 'quiet luxury'] into a TikTok caption for [your niche, e.g., 'sustainable fashion unboxing']: Hook with trend nod ('Quiet luxury, loud impact'), build interest with sensory details, desire via exclusivity, action as 'Duet this!'. 80 words max, youthful vibe with Gen Z slang. Output: Caption > Trend tie-in notes > Soundtrack pairing ideas."

4. User-Story Spotlight:

"Spotlight a customer story in an X (Twitter) thread caption for [testimonial, e.g., 'how our app saved a startup's launch']: Thread 4 tweets: Intro hook, journey arc, transformation reveal, grateful CTA. Use thread numeration, heartfelt tone. Format: Thread outline > Full text > Reply prompt for community (e.g., 'What's your win?')."

5. Humor-Hook Hybrid:

"Hybridize humor with value in a Facebook post caption for [tip, e.g., 'SEO myths busted']: Punny opener ('SEO: Search Engine Optimization or Secretly Eating Oreos?'), debunk 2 myths with facts, end with shareable laugh CTA. 120 words, witty brand voice. Output: Caption > Joke escalation table > Visual pairing (e.g., meme overlay)."

6. Seasonal Story Weaver:

"Weave a seasonal tie-in caption for Pinterest [holiday, e.g., 'Halloween productivity hacks']: Evoke festivity ('Pumpkin spice and all things sliced deadlines, that is'), list 3 themed tips, CTA to save/pin. Cozy tone, 100 words. Format: Sensory descriptors list > Caption > Pin title/alt-text suggestions."

7. Question-Cascade Creator:

"Create a question-cascade caption for YouTube Shorts [topic, e.g., 'AI tools for beginners']: Start with big query ('Struggling with AI overload?'), cascade to 3 sub-questions answered briefly, end with comment CTA. Energetic tone, 90 words. Output: Question flow diagram > Caption > Thumbnail text overlay ideas."

8. Behind-the-Scenes Bet:

"Bet on authenticity with a BTS caption for Instagram Reels [process, e.g., 'crafting your signature scent']: Tease vulnerability ('The failed batches that smelled like regret'), reveal the win, CTA to vote on next. 110 words, conversational voice. Format: Emotional arc notes > Caption > Story sticker integrations."

9. Value-Bomb Dropper:

"Drop a value bomb in a Reddit caption for [subreddit, e.g., r/Entrepreneur on 'scaling without burnout']: Explosive stat hook ('80% of founders burn out here's your shield'), 4 bullet insights, discussion CTA. Authoritative yet approachable, 140 words. Output: Bullet polish > Caption > Upvote bait phrases."

10. Collaborative Call-Out:

"Call out a collab in a multi-platform caption [partner, e.g., 'teaming with a fitness influencer for wellness tips']: Cross-shoutout hook ('When brains meet barbells...'), shared value pitch, joint CTA (e.g., 'DM us your mashup'). Inclusive tone, 100 words. Format: Platform adaptations > Caption template > Co-branded hashtag brainstorm."

2. LinkedIn Growth Prompts

LinkedIn is the professional arena for thought leadership and networking, where posts can expand your reach by 40% with consistent value-sharing (LinkedIn 2025 Insights). For beginners building visibility, these prompts focus on persona-driven content, SEO-optimized headlines, and engagement loops, crafting profiles and posts that position you as an expert without the sleaze.

Prompt :

1. Personal Brand Bio Builder:

"Build a compelling LinkedIn 'About' section for [your role, e.g., 'AI ethics consultant']: Hook with a bold opener ('I bridge code and conscience'), weave 3 career wins with stories, end with a collaboration invite. 2,600 chars max, first-person narrative. Output: Section draft > Keyword optimization list > Profile pic/header synergy tips."

2. Thought Leadership Post Crafter:

"Craft a LinkedIn article teaser post on [trend, e.g., '2026's AI regulations']: Provocative question hook, 3 key takeaways via bullets, CTA to read/comment. Professional tone, 200 words. Format: Post structure > Hashtag strategy (5 targeted) > Connection request template."

3. Networking Outreach Message:

"Draft a personalized LinkedIn connection request for [target, e.g., 'a VC in edtech']: Reference shared interest ('Loved your post on adaptive learning'), offer value (e.g., 'Here's a quick resource'), subtle follow-up ask. 300 chars, warm yet concise. Output: Message variants > Response anticipation > Follow-up sequence."

4. Milestone Celebration Post:

"Celebrate a career milestone [e.g., '10k followers'] on LinkedIn: Gratitude hook ('From solo coder to community catalyst'), reflect on lessons, tag influencers, CTA for shares. Inspirational tone, 150 words. Format: Emotional beats > Post copy > Visual element ideas (e.g., timeline infographic)."

5. Industry Insight Thread:

"Thread a LinkedIn series on [hot topic, e.g., 'remote work's hidden costs']: 5 connected posts—Stat intro, deep dive, counterpoint, solution, Q&A close. Analytical voice. Output: Thread map > Sample posts > Engagement metrics tracker."

6. Skill-Share Video Script:

"Script a short LinkedIn video caption for [skill, e.g., 'prompt engineering basics']: Tease value ('Unlock AI's potential in 60 seconds'), outline 3 steps, end with 'What's your hack?' 120 words, energetic tone. Format: Timestamped outline > Caption > Thumbnail prompt."

7. Endorsement Request Refiner:

"Refine a polite endorsement request message for [skill, e.g., 'strategic marketing']: Context hook ('Your insights shaped my last campaign'), specific ask, reciprocal offer. 200 chars. Output: Message > Timing tips > Relationship nurture plan."

8. Poll Powerhouse Post:

"Power a LinkedIn poll post on [dilemma, e.g., 'Hybrid vs. office work?']: Contextual intro with data, 4 options, analysis promise in comments. Curious tone, 100 words. Format: Poll setup > Follow-up comment template > Insight extraction guide."

9. Mentor Matchmaker Intro:

"Intro a mentorship offer post for [niche, e.g., 'aspiring SaaS founders']: Vulnerability share ('My first pivot flop taught me...'), 3 slots open, application CTA. Empowering voice. Output: Post draft > Screening questions > Success story add-on."

10. Year-in-Review Reflector:

"Reflect on a professional year-end post [achievements, e.g., 'From idea to $50k MRR']: Numbered wins, gratitude shoutouts, forward-looking goal. Reflective tone, 180 words. Format: Narrative arc > Visual timeline > Networking ripple effects."

3. Newsletter Writing Prompts

Newsletters are one of the most effective ways to build a loyal audience, especially in tech-focused communities where people appreciate useful insights, updates, and tools. A good newsletter feels like a trusted guide it consistently delivers value, helps readers learn something new, and keeps them coming back for more. For beginners, think of it as a longer, more personal version of a social media post. You choose a theme, share helpful information, add your perspective, and speak directly to your readers as if you're having a friendly conversation. Over time, this consistent value builds trust, strengthens your personal or brand identity, and creates a community that looks forward to hearing from you.

Whether you're writing tutorials, industry trends, coding tips, or product updates, the key is simple: make every edition worth your reader's time.

Prompt :

1. Curated Digest Designer:

"Design a newsletter edition on [theme, e.g., 'Python pitfalls to avoid']: Hook with a coder's anecdote ('That one-line bug that cost a weekend...'), curate 4 articles/resources with summaries, end with a hack CTA. 800 words, geeky yet accessible tone. Output: Sectioned layout > Link previews > Unsubscribe-proof value audit."

2. Story-Driven Starter:

"Start a newsletter story arc for [series, e.g., 'From novice to ninja: Week 1 JS journey']: Personal hook ('My first 'Hello World' flop'), 3 actionable steps with code snippets, reader challenge. Warm mentor voice, 600 words. Format: Narrative beats > Embedded code blocks > Poll for next topic."

3. Trend Breakdown Bulletin:

"Break down a coding trend [e.g., 'Rust's rise in web dev'] for [newsletter name]: Explainer intro, pros/cons table, 2 beginner experiments, subscribe CTA. Informative tone, 700 words. Output: Trend timeline > Resource round-up > A/B subject line tests."

4. Q&A Community Corner:

"Curate a Q&A newsletter from [audience queries, e.g., 'Best IDE for beginners?']: Aggregate 5 top questions, expert-style answers with pros, community shoutout. Collaborative vibe, 500 words. Format: Question-answer pairs > Visual poll results > Submission call-to-action."

5. Toolbox Teardown:

"Teardown a tool [e.g., 'VS Code extensions for productivity'] in a 'Smart Coding' issue: Benefit hook, step-by-step setup guide, real-user tip, upgrade path. Practical tone, 650 words. Output: Installation snippet > Comparison chart > Feedback loop prompt."

6. Failure-to-Fix Feature:

"Feature a coding failure story [e.g., 'My API meltdown and recovery'] for the newsletter: Relatable hook, root-cause analysis, 3 prevention tips, encouragement close. Vulnerable yet uplifting, 550 words. Format: Story arc > Code diff example > Reader share invite."

7. Roundup with Rankings:

"Rank and roundup [resources, e.g., 'Top 5 GitHub repos for ML newbies']: Criteria intro, numbered reviews with why/wow, exclusive discount if applicable. Enthusiastic tone, 750 words. Output: Ranking rubric > Snippet previews > Affiliate disclosure template."

8. Future-Focused Forecast:

"Forecast [tech shift, e.g., 'AI in everyday coding by 2026'] for 'Smart Coding': Speculative hook, 4 implications with examples, action steps, visionary close. Forward-thinking voice, 600 words. Format: Scenario branches > Expert quote pulls > Discussion thread starter."

9. Challenge Edition Igniter:

"Ignite a newsletter challenge [e.g., '30-day code streak starters']: Motivational opener, daily micro-tasks with templates, progress tracker, community join. Energizing tone, 700 words. Output: Calendar visual > Template links > Success story slot."

10. Deep Dive Decoder:

"Decode a complex concept [e.g., 'Quantum computing basics for coders'] simply: Analogy hook ('Like superposition in debugging?'), layered explanation, code analogy, Q&A teaser. Beginner-friendly expert, 650 words. Format: Analogy map > Simplified diagram description > Further reading curated list."

4. Product Descriptions Prompts

Product descriptions sell dreams through details, converting browsers to buyers with 25% higher carts when sensory and benefit-focused (BigCommerce 2025). For beginners, these prompts emphasize FAB (Features, Advantages, Benefits) structures and SEO keywords, helping you write copy that scans fast and sells deep iterate by reading aloud for flow.

Prompt :

1. Sensory Benefit Weaver:

"Weave a 150-word product description for [item, e.g., 'wireless noise-cancelling headphones']: Start with benefit hook ('Escape the chaos, dive into focus'), layer features (battery, fit) into advantages, end with urgency CTA. Vivid sensory language, conversational tone. Output: FAB breakdown > SEO keyword inserts > Bullet-point variant for e-com."

2. Story-Sold Spotlight:

"Spotlight [product, e.g., 'eco-leather journal'] via a 200-word mini-narrative: Hero's need ('In a digital flood, rediscover ink's magic'), product as savior, emotional close. Warm storytelling voice. Format: Arc outline > Description > User persona tie-in."

3. Comparison Converter:

"Convert skeptics with a 120-word description comparing [product, e.g., 'our smart blender vs. basics']: Highlight unique edges (app integration, durability), benefit pivot, buy-now nudge. Confident tone. Output: Vs. table snippet > Full copy > A/B price anchor ideas."

4. Eco-Ethos Endorser:

"Endorse sustainability in a 180-word description for [green product, e.g., 'bamboo toothbrush set']: Ethical hook ('Brush better for the planet'), material/features glow-up, guilt-free CTA. Purposeful voice. Format: Impact stats embed > Description > Certification badges prompt."

5. Tech-Spec Translator:

"Translate specs into sizzle for [gadget, e.g., '4K action cam']: Hook with use-case ('Capture the rush, frame by frame'), demystify features, benefit barrage. Geeky yet approachable, 160 words. Output: Jargon glossary > Copy > FAQ teaser section."

6. Lifestyle Linker:

"Link [product, e.g., 'yoga mat'] to lifestyle in 140-word description: Aspirational scene ('Roll out calm amid the storm'), seamless integration, transformative CTA. Inspirational tone. Format: Scene visualization > Description > Influencer collab angle."

7. Bundle Booster:

"Boost a bundle description [e.g., 'skincare starter kit'] at 170 words: Synergy hook ('More than pieces, your glow ritual'), individual shines + combo magic, limited-time CTA. Enthusiastic voice. Output: Bundle value calc > Copy > Upsell path suggestions."

8. Humor-Infused Highlight:

"Highlight [fun product, e.g., 'quirky desk plant pot'] with wit in 130 words: Playful pain point ('Say goodbye to sad desk salads'), feature fun, joyful buy-in. Lighthearted tone. Format: Pun ladder > Description > Meme-pairing ideas."

9. Luxury Lure:

"Lure with luxury for [premium item, e.g., 'handcrafted watch'] in 190 words: Sensory indulgence hook ('Time, wrapped in timeless elegance'), heritage details, exclusive CTA. Sophisticated voice. Output: Sensory map > Copy > Gifting personalization add-on."

10. Pain-Relief Pitch:

"Pitch relief for [solution product, e.g., 'back-support pillow'] in 150 words: Empathetic opener ('Neck kinks stealing your Netflix?'), targeted fixes, restorative close. Caring tone. Format: Problem-solution bridge > Description > Testimonial slot."

5. Business Strategy & Decision-Making Prompts

Business strategy is all about finding clarity when things feel uncertain, and for beginners, it can feel overwhelming to know where to start. This section breaks it down in a simple and practical way. Instead of treating strategy as something only experts can do, you'll learn how to turn broad ideas into clear action steps using easy tools like SWOT analysis and basic scenario planning. With the help of AI, you can quickly explore different possibilities, compare options, and reduce the chances of making risky decisions.

These prompts guide you to think logically about strengths, weaknesses, opportunities, and threats, then map out realistic plans you can actually follow. As you use them, check the outputs against your real goals or available data to see if they make sense. Over time, you'll build a sharper sense of direction and learn how to make decisions that move your business forward with confidence.

Prompt :

1. SWOT Strategy Synthesizer:

"Synthesize a SWOT analysis for [business move, e.g., 'launching a SaaS tool']: Brainstorm 4 points per quadrant with examples, derive 3 strategies from intersections. Balanced tone, 400 words. Output: Table format > Prioritized actions > Risk mitigation add-ons."

2. Scenario Planner:

"Plan 3 scenarios (optimistic, baseline, pessimistic) for [decision, e.g., 'expanding to Europe']: Chain causes/effects, assign probabilities, outline contingencies. Forward-looking voice. Format: Scenario matrix > Narrative summaries > Pivot triggers."

3. OKR Goal Aligner:

"Align OKRs for [quarterly focus, e.g., 'team productivity boost']: 3 Objectives with 4 Key Results each, tie to vision. Motivational tone, 300 words. Output: GSheet-ready table > Progress tracker template > Alignment audit questions."

4. Competitor Edge Auditor:

"Audit competitors [e.g., 'top 3 CRM tools'] for your edge: Map features/gaps, propose differentiators, SWOT crossover. Analytical voice. Format: Comparison chart > Strategy recommendations > Market share projections."

5. Pivot Decision Decoder:

"Decode a pivot decision [e.g., 'shift from B2C to B2B']: Pros/cons weighted list, stakeholder impacts, go/no-go criteria. Decisive tone, 350 words. Output: Decision tree text > Implementation timeline > Success KPI dashboard."

6. Resource Allocation Optimizer:

"Optimize resource allocation for [budget, e.g., '$50k marketing spend']: Pareto 80/20 breakdown, ROI estimates, reallocation rationale. Pragmatic voice. Format: Pie chart description > Allocation plan > Quarterly review prompts."

7. Innovation Brainstormer:

"Brainstorm innovations for [challenge, e.g., 'stagnant user growth']: SCAMPER on core product, rank 5 ideas by feasibility. Creative yet grounded, 400 words. Output: Idea matrix > Prototype outlines > Team vote simulator."

8. Crisis Response Crafter:

"Craft a crisis response strategy [e.g., 'data breach handling']: Timeline steps, comms plan, recovery metrics. Calm authority tone. Format: Phase-by-phase guide > Stakeholder map > Post-mortem template."

9. Partnership Pitch Planner:

"Plan a partnership pitch [e.g., 'co-marketing with a complementary brand']: Value prop, mutual wins, proposal structure. Collaborative voice, 300 words. Output: Pitch deck outline > Negotiation scripts > Deal-breaker checklist."

10. Long-Term Vision Backcaster:

"Backcast a 5-year vision [e.g., 'global scale-up'] to yearly milestones: Reverse-engineer steps, milestone metrics. Visionary tone. Format: Cascade diagram text > Annual goals > Adaptability flex points."

6. Sales Copy & Funnel Prompts

Sales copy is simply the art of guiding someone from curiosity to confidence, and eventually to a decision—and for beginners, this section makes that journey easy to understand. Instead of relying on complicated formulas, you'll learn clear and friendly methods like the PAS structure (Problem, Agitate, Solution), which helps you speak to real customer needs in a relatable way.

You'll also explore how to create simple nurture emails that build trust step by step, moving readers smoothly from awareness to interest and finally to taking action. With AI as your helper, you can personalize messages faster and more effectively, making your copy feel genuine instead of generic. As you practice, pay attention to open rates, click-throughs, and replies these small signals show what's resonating and help you refine your approach. By the end, you'll know how to write sales messages that feel human, helpful, and persuasive, even if you're just starting out.

Prompt :

1. Email Sequence Architect:

"Architect a 5-email nurture sequence for [lead magnet, e.g., 'e-book downloaders']: Email 1: Welcome/value deliver; 2-4: Pain agitation + tips; 5: Soft sell. Persuasive tone, 150 words/email. Output: Subject lines > Copy drafts > Automation tags."

2. Landing Page Persuader:

"Persuade on a landing page copy for [offer, e.g., 'free trial signup']: Hero hook (PAS opener), benefits bullets, social proof, urgency CTA. Benefit-focused voice, 400 words. Format: Section flow > Testimonials embed > A/B headline variants."

3. Objection Overcomer:

"Overcome objections [e.g., 'too expensive'] in sales copy: Empathize, reframe value, proof points, close question. Empathetic tone, 200 words. Output: Objection script > FAQ integration > Upsell bridge."

4. Webinar Invite Igniter:

"Ignite a webinar invite email [topic, e.g., 'Scaling startups with AI']: Tease transformation, agenda bullets, exclusive bonus CTA. Excited voice, 180 words. Format: Calendar hook > Copy > Follow-up reminder series."

5. Cart Abandonment Rescuer:

"Rescue cart abandoners with email copy [product, e.g., 'abandoned sneakers']: Reminder hook, discount nudge, easy checkout CTA. Friendly urgency, 120 words. Output: Personalization fields > Copy > Retargeting ad tie-in."

6. Testimonial Transformer:

"Transform testimonials into sales snippets for [funnel stage, e.g., 'consideration page']: Curate 3 quotes with context, weave into narrative. Trust-building tone, 250 words. Format: Quote carousel > Integration spots > Fresh testimonial prompt."

7. Upsell Opportunity Opener:

"Open an upsell email post-purchase [add-on, e.g., 'premium features']: Congratulate, highlight synergy, limited-time offer. Grateful voice, 160 words. Output: Trigger timing > Copy > Churn prevention notes."

8. Cold Outreach Customizer:

"Customize cold sales email [prospect, e.g., 'e-com store owner']: Research hook, tailored pain solve, meeting CTA. Respectful tone, 140 words. Output: Personalization checklist > Copy > Response nurture path."

9. Funnel Flow Mapper:

"Map a full funnel copy audit [e.g., 'awareness to loyalty']: Identify drop-offs, rewrite 3 key touchpoints with PAS. Diagnostic voice, 350 words. Format: Funnel diagram text > Revised copies > Conversion uplift estimates."

10. Close-the-Deal Closer:

"Close with high-ticket sales copy [e.g., 'consulting package pitch']: Scarcity hook, ROI proof, one-question objection buster, sign-now CTA. Confident tone, 220 words. Output: Psychological triggers > Copy > Contract follow-up script."

Chapter 7 Education & Learning Prompts

Learning can feel overwhelming when there's too much information and not enough clarity, but this chapter is designed to make the process simple, calm, and deeply effective for beginners. Think of AI as a friendly study partner one that helps you understand difficult topics faster, ask better questions, and stay engaged instead of getting stuck. Here, you'll explore easy-to-use prompting techniques inspired by proven learning methods like the Feynman technique (explaining things in simple words), Socratic questioning (breaking ideas down through guided questions), and spaced-repetition reminders (reinforcing what you've learned over time). Instead of memorizing facts, you'll learn to interact actively with the material: ask the AI to simplify concepts, check your understanding, test your recall, and help you build personalized explanations that truly click. These prompts work across all AI models and are structured to give you clear, precise, and helpful answers every time.

Across five areas clear explanations, tutor-like guidance, step-by-step learning paths, quick self-quizzes, and easy revision notes you'll discover how to turn studying into a smooth and rewarding experience. Whether you're exploring science, improving your coding skills, or trying to understand a new concept from scratch, this chapter helps you learn smarter, not harder.

1. Explain Anything Simplified

Explaining complex ideas simply is the art of the educator, stripping away jargon to reveal core truths like turning a labyrinth into a lighted trail. In 2025, AI-driven simplifications boost retention by 35% in online courses (Coursera analytics), empowering beginners to grasp giants like relativity or recursion without intimidation. These prompts invoke the Feynman method (teach as if to a child) and analogies (bridging known to new), with constraints for brevity ideal for quick "aha" moments.

Prompt:

1. Feynman Analogy Builder:

"As a master explainer like Richard Feynman, simplify [topic, e.g., 'blockchain basics'] for a 10-year-old: Start with a everyday analogy (e.g., 'like a shared toy box where everyone checks entries'), break into 3 core steps with fun examples, end with a 'why it matters' hook. Limit to 200 words, vivid language. Output: Analogized sections > Quick quiz question > Common misconception flag."

2. Jargon-to-Joy Translator:

"Translate [concept, e.g., 'neural networks'] into joyful prose: Avoid tech terms by swapping with metaphors (e.g., 'brain cells chatting at a party'), layer 4 building blocks progressively, tie to real-life win (e.g., 'powers your photo filters'). 150 words max, enthusiastic tone. Format: Metaphor map > Simplified narrative > Visual aid suggestion (e.g., doodle prompt)."

3. Myth-Busting Breakdown:

"Bust myths in explaining [idea, e.g., 'evolution by natural selection']: Counter 2 common errors upfront (e.g., 'Not just survival of the fittest it's adaptation'), explain mechanism via 3 evidence-based steps, conclude with wonder factor. Conversational voice, 250 words. Output: Myth table > Step-by-step flow > Extension reading nudge."

4. Historical Hook Unpacker:

"Unpack [historical scientific idea, e.g., 'Newton's laws'] with a timeline hook: Weave discovery story (e.g., 'Apple-falling epiphany'), simplify each law with household demo, link to modern magic (e.g., 'Why your phone doesn't fly off'). 180 words, narrative flair. Format: Timeline bullets > Law analogies > Experiment at-home idea."

5. Everyday Echo Explainer:

"Echo [abstract concept, e.g., 'supply and demand'] in daily life: Hook with scenario ('Your coffee craving at rush hour'), dissect curve shifts with 2 examples, reveal personal impact (e.g., 'Prices you pay'). Relatable tone, 160 words. Output: Scenario sketch > Core mechanic > Decision-making tie-in question."

6. Visual Verbose-to-Vivid:

"Vividly simplify [technical term, e.g., 'photosynthesis'] without diagrams paint pictures: Sensory walkthrough (e.g., 'Leaves sipping sunlight like a green smoothie'), 3 phase breakdown, eco-connection close. Poetic yet precise, 200 words. Format: Sensory layers > Phase table > Nature walk reflection prompt."

7. Counterintuitive Clarity Crafter:

"Craft clarity for [counterintuitive fact, e.g., 'quantum entanglement']: Acknowledge weirdness ('Spooky action at distance?'), analogy chain (e.g., 'Twin dice always matching'), 4 key implications. Curious tone, 170 words. Output: Weirdness scale > Analogy chain > Sci-fi link (e.g., 'Like telepathy in stories')."

8. Build-from-Basics Builder:

"Build [skill, e.g., 'basic algebra'] from zero: Assume no prior knowledge, stack 3 foundational bricks with toy problems, celebrate small win. Encouraging voice, 220 words. Format: Brick pyramid > Solved examples > Next-level teaser."

9. Cultural Context Clarifier:

"Clarify [global concept, e.g., 'democracy's origins'] through cultural lens: Hook with diverse example (e.g., 'From Athens agora to town hall chats'), unpack pillars with cross-culture nods, relevance today. Inclusive tone, 190 words. Output: Culture comparisons > Pillar bullets > Debate starter question."

10. Humor-Infused Illuminator:

"Illuminate [dense topic, e.g., 'string theory'] with laughs: Punny entry ('Strings pulling the universe's puppet show?'), demystify via 3 goofy analogies, end on awe. Witty voice, 150 words. Format: Joke setup > Core unpack > Mind-bender follow-up."

2. Tutor-Style Prompts

Tutor-style interactions recreate the feeling of having a patient, one-on-one mentor who guides you step by step, helping you understand a topic instead of rushing you through it. These prompts are perfect for beginners because they encourage the AI to act like a supportive tutor, asking gentle questions, checking your understanding, and giving hints rather than just handing over the answer. This approach mirrors the Socratic method, where learning happens through curiosity and guided discovery rather than memorization. By interacting with the AI in this way, you build confidence, strengthen problem-solving skills, and develop a clearer grasp of the subject. It becomes less about cramming information and more about truly understanding the “why” behind each idea.

Prompt :

1. Socratic Question Cascade:

"Role-play as a Socratic tutor for [subject, e.g., 'intro to philosophy']: Pose 5 escalating questions on [key idea, e.g., 'Socrates' method'], respond to my hypothetical answers with probes/clarifications, end with self-reflection prompt. Adaptive tone, interactive format. Output: Question tree > Sample dialogue branch > Confidence booster tip."

2. Debugging Dialogue Guide:

"Guide me as a coding tutor through [bug scenario, e.g., 'Python loop not iterating']: Ask diagnostic questions (e.g., 'What's your input?'), suggest 2-3 fixes with why, simulate my trial-and-error. Supportive voice. Format: Step Q&A > Code snippet examples > 'Eureka' celebration phrase."

3. Concept Connection Coach:

"Coach connections as a history tutor for [event, e.g., 'French Revolution']: Link to [personal hook, e.g., 'modern protests'], quiz with 3 bridging questions, expand on answers. Engaging tone, 300 words per exchange. Output: Connection web > Follow-up query > Timeline tie-in visual idea."

4. Math Mindset Mentor:

"Mentor mindset for [math challenge, e.g., 'solving quadratics']: Empathize with frustration, break into visual steps (e.g., 'Graph as a parabola party'), pose practice with hints. Encouraging voice. Format: Hurdle-overcoming script > Worked example > Growth affirmation."

5. Language Nuance Nudger:

"Nudge nuances as a language tutor for [phrase, e.g., 'idioms in Spanish']: Contextualize with story, drill with 4 usage scenarios, correct gently via questions. Cultural flair, interactive. Output: Scenario dialogues > Nuance table > Conversation practice prompt."

6. Science Skeptic Simulator:

"Simulate a science tutor addressing skepticism on [theory, e.g., 'climate change models']: Counter doubts with evidence Qs, build buy-in via experiments, affirm curiosity. Balanced tone. Format: Doubt-debunk chain > Evidence links > Ethical implication question."

7. Creative Critiquer:

"Critique creatively as an art tutor for [sketch idea, e.g., 'urban fantasy scene']: Praise strengths, suggest 3 enhancements via 'what if' prompts, iterate on feedback. Inspirational voice. Output: Feedback sandwich > Revision sketch notes > Portfolio reflection."

8. Economics Everyday Explainer:

"Explain economics tutor-style for [principle, e.g., 'opportunity cost']: Relate to daily choice (e.g., 'Coffee or cram?'), probe trade-offs with scenarios, summarize insight. Practical tone. Format: Choice matrix > Scenario role-play > Budgeting application."

9. Lit Layer Peeler:

"Peel layers as a literature tutor for [text, e.g., 'Shakespeare sonnet']: Unpack symbols via questions, connect to emotions, suggest rewrite twist. Interpretive voice. Output: Symbol onion > Emotional echo > Modern adaptation idea."

10. Wellness Wisdom Walker:

"Walk through wellness as a tutor for [habit, e.g., 'mindful breathing']: Demo via guided steps, check-in questions, adapt to barriers. Calm tone. Format: Breath sequence > Barrier brainstorm > Journal prompt for tracking."

3. Step-by-Step Learning Paths

Step-by-step learning paths act like a reliable GPS for building new skills, breaking big, overwhelming goals into clear and manageable milestones. This approach is especially helpful for beginners because it removes the guesswork showing exactly what to learn first, what comes next, and how each step connects to the bigger picture. With AI's ability to organize information and tailor guidance, these structured paths help learners progress faster and more confidently, offering personalized checkpoints, recommended resources, and gentle nudges along the way. Instead of feeling lost or unsure where to start, you get a simple, guided roadmap that keeps you moving forward, one achievable step at a time.

Prompt :

1. Beginner Blueprint Crafter:

"Craft a 6-week learning path for [skill, e.g., 'web development basics']: Week 1: Foundations (e.g., HTML intro); include daily 30-min tasks, weekly quiz, resources (free sites). Motivational milestones. Output: Weekly table (goals > activities > checks) > Resource links > Pace adjustment tips."

2. Project-Paced Pathfinder:

"Path a project-based plan for [goal, e.g., 'build a simple app']: 5 phases from ideation to deploy, with sub-steps and tools (e.g., GitHub). Hands-on focus. Format: Phase flowchart text > Milestone deliverables > Troubleshooting sidebar."

3. Theory-to-Practice Trail:

"Trail from theory to practice for [topic, e.g., 'machine learning intro']: 8 steps blending reads/videos with exercises, spaced reviews. Balanced progression. Output: Step ladder > Practice prompts > Retention hook (e.g., teach-back)."

4. Interdisciplinary Integration Itinerary:

"Itinerary an interdisciplinary path [e.g., 'data viz + storytelling']: Merge fields in 7 modules, cross-apply via mini-projects. Creative tone. Format: Module matrix > Fusion examples > Peer review idea."

5. Habit-Honed Highway:

"Highway a habit-integrated path for [language, e.g., 'conversational French']: Daily immersion steps, weekly immersion challenges, app trackers. Sustainable voice. Output: Habit calendar > Immersion log > Plateau buster strategies."

6. Advanced Anchor Adjuster:

"Adjust a path for advancing beginners in [field, e.g., 'photography composition']: 10 steps from rules to rule-breaking, with critiques. Exploratory tone. Format: Anchor points > Critique rubric > Gallery inspiration."

7. Resource-Rich Roadmap:

"Roadmap with resources for [cert, e.g., 'Google Analytics beginner']: Curate free/paid per step, 4-week sprint, assessment gates. Efficient voice. Output: Resource tiers > Sprint timeline > Cert sim quiz link."

8. Collaborative Climb Chart:

"Chart a collaborative path [e.g., 'team coding project']: Group steps with roles, sync points, feedback loops. Inclusive tone. Format: Climb diagram > Role assignments > Conflict resolution tips."

9. Reflection-Routed Route:

"Route with reflections for [philosophy self-study]: 6 thematic steps, journal prompts per milestone, synthesis capstone. Introspective voice. Output: Reflection stations > Journal template > Insight harvest question."

10. Gamified Growth Guide:

"Guide gamified learning for [game dev basics]: Level-up steps with badges (e.g., 'Sprite Master'), challenges, score trackers. Fun tone. Format: Level map > Badge criteria > Replay motivation."

4. Quiz / Test Generator

Quizzes are more than quick memory checks, they help you understand how prepared you really are, revealing both strengths and areas that need more practice. With today's AI tools able to personalize questions based on your performance, learners often see noticeable improvements because the quiz adapts to what they need most. For beginners, this makes studying far less stressful and far more effective. You can create different types of questions like multiple choice for quick checks or open-ended questions for deeper thinking and get instant feedback that keeps you on track. By using quizzes this way, you're not just testing what you know; you're building confidence and reinforcing your learning in a clear, supportive, and structured way.

Prompt :

1. Multiple-Choice Mastery Maker:

"Make a 10-question MCQ quiz on [topic, e.g., 'basic biology cells']: 4 options each, one correct; include distractors from misconceptions. Beginner level. Output: Numbered questions > Answer key with explanations > Score rubric."

2. Open-Ended Odyssey:

"Odyssey an 8-question open-ended test for [skill, e.g., 'essay writing tips']: Prompts probing depth, rubrics for grading. Thoughtful voice. Format: Question set > Holistic rubric > Sample strong response."

3. Scenario-Based Simulator:

"Simulate 6 scenario quizzes for [field, e.g., 'ethical dilemmas in business']: Real-world cases, choose-your-path branches. Ethical tone. Output: Branching paths > Decision tree > Debrief discussion."

4. Flashcard Flip Quiz:

"Flip a 15-card quiz for [vocab, e.g., 'Spanish greetings']: Front/back with hints, spaced order. Memorable voice. Format: Card deck > Usage examples > Review algorithm suggestion."

5. True/False Trapper:

"Trap truths in a 12 T/F quiz on [myth-heavy topic, e.g., 'nutrition facts']: Explain falses with corrections. Clarifying tone. Output: Statement list > Justification pairs > Myth-bust bonus."

6. Matching Mastery Match:

"Match 10 pairs for [concepts, e.g., 'programming paradigms']: Terms to definitions, shuffleable. Associative voice. Format: Matching grid > Key > Extension pairing game."

7. Fill-in-the-Blank Filler:

"Fill 9 blanks in sentences for [grammar, e.g., 'English tenses']: Contextual clues, varied difficulty. Precise tone. Output: Cloze exercises > Completions with rationale > Pattern spotter."

8. Diagram Labeler:

"Label a diagram quiz for [visual topic, e.g., 'heart anatomy']: Describe image, 7 hotspots to tag. Visual voice. Format: Description prompt > Label key > Sketch alternative."

9. Peer-Review Prepper:

"Prep a 5-essay peer-review quiz [e.g., 'peer feedback on arguments']: Rubric-guided questions. Collaborative tone. Output: Review framework > Sample feedback > Self-assess mirror."

10. Adaptive Assessment Architect:

"Architect an adaptive quiz on [progressive skill, e.g., 'algebra basics to advanced']: 12 questions, branch on answers. Dynamic voice. Format: Flowchart > Question bank > Personalization notes."

5. Revision Notes Generator

Revision notes take complex information and break it down into simple, memorable pieces that are easy to review anytime. Instead of sifting through long chapters or heavy explanations, well-crafted notes highlight only what truly matters key ideas, definitions, examples, and connections. With modern AI tools helping learners summarize and organize material, many people find they can review nearly twice as effectively while spending far less time. For beginners especially, good revision notes act like a friendly roadmap: they're clear, scannable, and designed to trigger active recall, which is one of the strongest ways to strengthen memory. Whether you're preparing for an exam, learning a new topic, or revisiting something after a break, these prompts help you create summaries that simplify even dense subjects, making your study sessions lighter, faster, and much more enjoyable.

Prompt :

1. Mind-Map Maker:

"Make revision notes as a mind map for [chapter, e.g., 'World War II causes']: Central node with 5 branches, mnemonics per leaf (e.g., 'Treaty, Versailles = TV drama'). Visual text format. Output: ASCII map > Mnemonic glossary > Quiz tie-in."

2. Bullet Bliss Condenser:

"Condense [lecture notes, e.g., 'photosynthesis process'] into 1-page bullets: Hierarchy (main > sub > examples), bold keywords, 200 words. Scannable tone. Format: Themed sections > Highlight reel > Flashcard conversion."

3. Timeline Treasure Trove:

"Trove a timeline of notes for [history arc, e.g., 'Renaissance inventions']: Key dates/events with impacts, visual icons described. Chronological voice. Output: Linear timeline > Impact bubbles > Connection web."

4. Formula Fortress Builder:

"Build a fortress of notes for [math formulas, e.g., 'trigonometry identities']: Each with derivation sketch, application example, cheat-sheet layout. Logical tone. Format: Formula cards > Deriv mini-steps > Problem solver."

5. Vocab Vault Visualizer:

"Visualizer vocab notes for [terms, e.g., 'literary devices']: Word > definition > example sentence > synonym/antonym. Thematic groups. Output: Vault categories > Sentence starters > Usage quiz."

6. Concept Cluster Condensor:

"Cluster concepts in notes for [science unit, e.g., 'atomic structure']: Interlinked bubbles with pros/cons, diagram descriptions. Integrative voice. Format: Cluster diagram text > Link legends > Analogy anchors."

7. Case Study Capsule:

"Capsule case studies in notes for [business examples, e.g., 'marketing fails']: Summary > lessons > visuals suggested. Narrative tone. Output: Case capsules > Lesson takeaways > Strategy apply prompt."

8. Language Layered Ledger:

"Ledger layered notes for [grammar rules, e.g., 'French verb conjugations']: Tables by tense, exceptions highlighted, practice phrases. Structured voice. Format: Conjugation grids > Exception alerts > Dialogue drill."

9. Philosophy Pearl Polisher:

"Polish philosophy notes as pearls for [thinker, e.g., 'Nietzsche's ideas']: Quote > interpretation > counterpoint, thematic thread. Reflective tone. Output: Pearl string > Debate sparks > Modern relevance."

10. Health Habit Harbinger:

"Harbinger health notes for [topic, e.g., 'nutrition basics']: Fact > myth bust > tip > tracker template. Empowering voice. Format: Habit harbors > Tracker chart > Weekly win log."

Chapter 8

Image + Video + Audio Prompts

Multimodal AI, like Google's Gemini, brings together different types of information such as text, images, audio, and video, making it easier to understand and work with real-world content. Instead of relying only on text inputs, you can upload a photo, a clip, or even a voice note, and Gemini can analyze it, explain it, or build something new from it. This makes learning and creating much faster and more natural, especially for beginners who want clear insights without technical steps. In this chapter, you'll explore how to use Gemini's multimodal abilities to understand images, transcribe audio, break down videos, and combine different media into powerful workflows. You'll also learn simple techniques like asking follow-up questions, adding emotional or contextual cues, and refining outputs to make your prompts more effective over time.

Everything here is built around the ICCEF method, which helps you give the model clear instructions with context and examples. You don't need coding knowledge; just upload your media, add a thoughtful prompt, check whether the result feels accurate or helpful, and adjust as needed. Whether you're a creator, a student, or someone exploring AI for the first time, this chapter shows how multimodal tools can turn everyday content into meaningful, well-organized insights.

1. Prompting Gemini with Images

Images capture moments filled with meaning, and with Gemini's visual abilities, you can explore those moments in a clear and thoughtful way. Instead of just looking at a picture, you can ask Gemini to describe what's happening, identify objects, understand emotions, or even explain the scene in a deeper cultural or creative context. This makes it especially helpful for beginners who may not know where to start when analyzing an image. The best approach is simple: upload your image first, then ask a straightforward question like "What's in this picture?" From there, you can build up to more detailed prompts, such as asking for mood analysis, design critiques, or storytelling ideas. Whether you're a designer wanting feedback on a visual, a student studying artwork, or someone simply curious about a photo, these prompts help you uncover layers you might miss turning a single image into a richer, more insightful experience.

Prompt :

1. Visual Description Decoder:

"As a museum curator, describe this uploaded image [reference the image] in vivid detail: Foreground elements first (e.g., 'a weathered hand clutching a faded letter'), then midground and background, noting colors, textures, and implied motion. Constrain to 150 words, sensory-rich language. Output: Layered paragraphs (front/mid/back) > Mood inference (e.g., 'melancholic nostalgia') > One creative extension (e.g., 'What letter might it hold?')."

2. Object Detection:

"Act as a forensic analyst scanning this image for objects: List 5-7 key items with positions (e.g., 'center: antique clock at 2 o'clock'), estimate interactions (e.g., 'shadow suggests recent use'), and flag anomalies. Beginner-friendly explanations, 200 words max. Format: Bulleted inventory > Interaction map (text sketch) > Practical tip (e.g., 'For photography: Balance composition')."

3. Sentiment Style Scanner:

"Scan this image for emotional tone as an art therapist: Assign a primary sentiment (e.g., 'serene isolation') with evidence (colors, poses), suggest 3 viewer interpretations. Chain to cultural lens if applicable. Warm, empathetic tone, 180 words. Output: Sentiment spectrum table > Interpretation branches > Therapeutic prompt (e.g., 'Journal what this evokes in you')."

4. Composition Critique Coach:

"Coach composition as a photography tutor: Analyze rule adherence (e.g., 'Golden ratio leads eye to subject'), strengths/weaknesses, 2 improvement tweaks. Upload assumes portrait; constrain to positive framing. Output: Rule-by-rule breakdown > Before/after sketch ideas > Beginner exercise (e.g., 'Recrop this mentally')."

5. Historical Hypothetizer:

"Hypothesize historical context for this image (e.g., 'vintage photo'): Infer era via clues (clothing, tech), weave a 100-word backstory, rate confidence (1-10). Narrative voice. Format: Clue list > Fictional vignette > Fact-check nudge (e.g., 'Cross-reference with era databases')."

6. Color Harmony Harmonizer:

"Harmonize colors in this image as a designer: Palette extraction (top 5 hues), harmony type (e.g., analogous), mood tie-in, suggest edits for accessibility. Vibrant tone, 160 words. Output: Swatch description > Harmony analysis > Edit palette variants (e.g., 'Monochrome for drama')."

7. Symbolism Storyteller:

"Storytell symbols in this artwork/image: Identify 3-4 (e.g., 'broken chain = liberation'), link to themes, craft a micro-narrative. Interpretive yet grounded, 200 words. Format: Symbol table > Narrative weave > Personal reflection question."

8. Accessibility Auditor:

"Audit accessibility as an inclusive designer: Check contrast ratios, alt-text potential, 3 fixes for color-blind users. Supportive voice. Output: Compliance checklist > Suggested alt-text > Inclusive redesign prompt."

9. Trend Tie-In Tracker:

"Track trends in this fashion/lifestyle image: Spot 4 elements (e.g., 'oversized silhouettes'), link to 2025 vibes, predict evolution. Trendy tone, 150 words. Format: Element spotlight > Trend forecast > Styling inspiration (e.g., 'Pair with...')."

10. Emotional Echo Explorer:

"Explore emotional echoes in this landscape: Evoke feelings via weather/lighting (e.g., 'Stormy skies = inner turmoil'), suggest 2 artistic inspirations. Poetic voice, 170 words. Output: Echo layers > Inspiration refs (e.g., 'Turner seascapes') > Mood board extension."

2. Gemini for Audio Transcription

Audio captures real, unfiltered moments whether it's a conversation, a lecture, a voice note, or a song. Gemini's transcription tools make it easy to turn these sounds into clear, readable text, even when the recording isn't perfect. This is especially helpful for beginners who want to focus on understanding the content rather than manually typing everything out. The simplest way to start is to upload your audio file and ask Gemini to create a clean transcript. Once you're comfortable with that, you can move on to deeper analysis, like identifying different speakers, highlighting key ideas, summarizing long sections, or pulling out action points. These kinds of prompts are great for podcasters preparing episode summaries, students reviewing class recordings, or anyone who wants to quickly make sense of spoken information. With a single upload, your audio becomes easier to study, reference, and build upon turning sound into insight.

Prompt :

1. Clean Transcript Crafter:

"Transcribe this uploaded audio [reference file] verbatim: Timestamp every 30 seconds, note pauses/fillers (e.g., '[hesitation]'), format as dialogue if multi-speaker. Accurate and neutral, full length. Output: Timestamped script > Speaker tags (if detected) > Summary skim (100 words)."

2. Themed Annotation Adder:

"Transcribe and annotate this podcast clip for [theme, e.g., 'AI ethics']: Highlight 5 key quotes with context, add theme ties (e.g., 'Echoes Bostrom's warnings'). Concise notes, 80% transcript/20% analysis. Format: Annotated sections > Quote pull-list > Actionable takeaway."

3. Speaker Sentiment Sifter:

"Sift speakers in this audio for sentiments: Transcribe core dialogue, tag emotions per turn (e.g., 'excited: rising pitch'), summarize arc. Empathetic tone. Output: Dialogue with tags > Sentiment timeline > Insight (e.g., 'Tension peaks at 2:15')."

4. Lecture Learning Locker:

"Lock in a lecture transcript with learning aids: Full text, bold key terms, 3 bullet summaries per section, quiz questions. Educational voice. Format: Sectioned transcript > Term glossary > 5-question recap."

5. Song Lyric Layerer:

"Layer lyrics from this song audio: Transcribe verses/chorus with timestamps, note rhyme schemes, interpret metaphors. Musical tone, 200 words analysis. Output: Structured lyrics > Scheme breakdown > Theme mood board."

6. Interview Insight Extractor:

"Extract insights from this interview: Transcribe Q&A, highlight gems (e.g., 'Gold nugget: Pivot mindset'), suggest follow-ups. Curatorial voice. Format: Q&A pairs > Insight bullets > Research prompt (e.g., 'Verify stat at 4:20')."

7. Accent Adaptation Assistant:

"Adapt for accents in this non-native audio: Transcribe phonetically where needed (e.g., 'thuh' for 'the'), clarify ambiguities, add glossary. Inclusive tone. Output: Adapted script > Phonetic guide > Comprehension check questions."

8. Noise-Reduction Narrator:

"Narrate a clean transcript from noisy audio: Filter background, focus on speech, note interruptions. Precise voice. Format: Polished text > Noise log > Enhanced version comparison."

9. Motivational Message Miner:

"Mine motivational peaks in this speech: Transcribe highlights, amp rhetoric (e.g., 'Anaphora builds urgency'), craft remix snippet. Inspiring tone, 150 words. Output: Peak excerpts > Rhetoric analysis > Personal application."

10. Multilingual Magic Mapper:

"Map a bilingual audio transcript: Transcribe in original + English, note code-switches, cultural nuances. Global voice. Format: Dual-column script > Switch highlights > Translation fidelity notes."

3. Prompting for Video Analysis

Videos blend movement, sound, and emotion into a single experience, and Gemini helps you break down that complexity in a clear, approachable way. Instead of scrubbing through clips frame by frame, beginners can simply upload a video and ask Gemini to summarize what's happening, identify key moments, or explain the overall mood. Once you're comfortable with the basics, you can dive deeper exploring pacing, character behavior, visual motifs, or even how well the video communicates its message. This makes the tool incredibly useful for creators, marketers, educators, or anyone working with video content.

Whether you're analyzing a tutorial, evaluating a vlog, or studying a short film, these prompts help you understand what works, what doesn't, and how the visuals come together to tell a story. With Gemini, every clip becomes easier to interpret, refine, and learn from, turning video analysis into a simple and powerful creative skill.

Prompt :

1. Scene Summary Storyteller:

"Storytell a summary of this video [reference upload]: Break into 3-5 scenes with timestamps (e.g., '0:00-1:30: Intro hook'), note visual/ audio cues, overall arc. Narrative tone, 250 words. Output: Timestamped acts > Arc diagram (text) > Hook strength rating."

2. Pacing Pulse Checker:

"Check pacing in this tutorial video: Transcribe key beats, flag drags/ rushes (e.g., '2x speed at demos'), suggest trims. Instructional voice. Format: Beat timeline > Pace graph description > Edit timeline proposal."

3. Emotion Evolution Explorer:

"Explore emotion flow in this vlog: Frame-sample sentiments (e.g., 'Joy spikes at laugh track'), trace arc via music/poses, peak moments. Empathetic tone, 200 words. Output: Emotion curve > Peak clips > Viewer empathy tip."

4. Motif Motion Mapper:

"Map motifs in this narrative video (e.g., 'recurring red door'): Timestamp appearances, symbolic ties, narrative role. Analytical voice. Format: Motif log > Symbol web > Remix idea (e.g., 'Color-grade for emphasis')."

5. Accessibility Angle Auditor:

"Audit accessibility in this explainer: Transcribe captions, check visual clarity/audio sync, 3 inclusive fixes. Supportive tone. Output: Compliance checklist > Caption gaps > Alt-audio suggestions."

6. Trend Trace Tracker:

"Track trends in this ad video: Spot 4 elements (e.g., 'TikTok-style cuts'), link to 2025 vibes, engagement forecast. Trendy voice, 180 words. Format: Element timestamps > Trend forecast > Viral tweak (e.g., 'Add AR filter')."

7. Character Dynamic Decoder:

"Decode character dynamics in this dialogue video: Transcribe exchanges, analyze power shifts via body language, relationship arc. Psychological tone. Output: Exchange pairs > Dynamic chart > Casting insight."

8. Soundscape Symphony Synthesizer:

"Synthesize soundscape in this ambient video: Layer audio elements (e.g., 'Foley crunches at 1:45'), mood contribution, remix proposal. Auditory voice. Format: Layer breakdown > Mood map > Foley enhancement prompt."

9. Frame-by-Frame Forensicator:

"Forensicate key frames in this action clip: Select 5 pivotal (e.g., 'Impact at 3:20'), detail composition/motion, tension build. Cinematic tone, 220 words. Output: Frame gallery descriptions > Tension build > Slow-mo edit idea."

10. Narrative Nuance Nudger:

"Nudge narrative nuances in this story video: Transcribe plot points, subtle foreshadowing, ending twist potential. Interpretive voice. Format: Point timeline > Nuance highlights > Alternate ending brainstorm."

4. Advanced Multimodal Workflows

Advanced multimodal workflows let you combine images, videos, and audio to create richer, more meaningful insights almost like blending different art forms into one cohesive story. Instead of treating each file separately, you learn to connect them: a photo can set the mood, a video can provide context, and an audio clip can add emotion or narrative depth. For beginners, this process becomes easier when you tackle it step by step. First, upload all the media you want to use. Then you prompt Gemini in a simple sequence start by asking for a breakdown of each piece, move on to combining the insights, and finally refine the output into something polished and useful. This approach builds confidence while showing how different media can work together to enhance storytelling, teaching, or content creation.

It's especially helpful for educators preparing lessons, creators planning content, or marketers building campaigns. With these guided prompts, multimodal workflows become an accessible way to produce deeper, more engaging results without feeling overwhelming.

Prompt :

1. Travel Tale Weaver:

"Weave a multimodal travel recap: From uploaded video (narrative arc), image (visual highlights), audio (ambient sounds) craft 300-word story with timestamps, sensory fusion. Adventurous tone. Output: Fused timeline > Sensory blend > Itinerary remix."

2. Recipe Remix Remixer:

"Remix a cooking video workflow: Transcribe audio instructions, analyze image ingredients, video steps & generate simplified script with visuals. Culinary voice, 250 words. Format: Step fusion > Ingredient map > Dietary adaptation."

3. Fitness Flow Fusion:

"Fuse fitness routine: Video poses analysis, audio cues transcription, image before/after build progress guide with tips. Motivational tone. Output: Pose sequence > Cue timeline > Personalization prompt."

4. Art Critique Cascade:

"Cascade an art critique: Image style breakdown, video creation process transcript, audio artist interview. Synthesize 200-word review. Critical voice. Format: Modality layers > Synthesis essay > Exhibition pitch."

5. Podcast-to-Visualizer Pipeline:

"Pipeline a podcast episode: Audio transcript themes, paired image mood board, video clip highlights create episode graphic with quotes. Creative tone. Output: Theme visuals > Quote cards > Promo reel idea."

6. Event Echo Enhancer:

"Enhance event recap: Video highlights, image candids, audio cheers narrate 280-word montage script. Celebratory voice. Format: Echo montage > Emotional peaks > Invite follow-up."

7. Tutorial Triple Threat:

"Triple-threat a DIY tutorial: Video demo steps, image tool close-ups, audio narration— efine into beginner guide with warnings. Practical tone, 220 words. Output: Integrated steps > Tool glossary > Safety checklist."

8. Music Video Mood Mapper:

"Map moods in a music video workflow: Audio lyrics sentiment, video visuals sync, image album art propose remix. Harmonic voice. Format: Sync timeline > Mood fusion > Fan edit concept."

9. Therapy Session Synthesizer:

"Synthesize a mock therapy insight: Audio dialogue transcript, video body language, image emotion chart offer reflective summary. Gentle tone, 250 words. Output: Insight layers > Reflection questions > Privacy note."

10. Brand Story Blender:

"Blend a brand story: Video ad analysis, image logo mood, audio tagline craft unified narrative pitch. Strategic voice. Format: Story blender > Unified script > Campaign extension (e.g., social series)."

Chapter 9
Advanced Prompting Techniques

Advanced prompting is where everyday questions begin to feel more like guided conversations clear, structured, and designed to bring out the deepest reasoning an AI can offer. Instead of seeing prompting as just typing instructions, this chapter helps beginners understand how to shape the flow of thought behind an AI's response. You'll learn practical techniques such as chain-of-thought (breaking problems into clear steps), multi-agent prompting (letting the AI simulate different perspectives), recursive prompting (refining ideas through repeated passes), role-stacking (giving the AI layered personas to improve depth), meta-prompts (teaching the model to refine its own output), and long-context prompting (handling large stories or complex tasks). These approaches aren't complicated tricks they're simple methods that build on each other.

You start with a basic question, review the AI's answer to see if it explains the why, and then guide it with small additions or constraints to sharpen the results. The prompts in this chapter follow a clear framework to help you stay consistent and get reliable outputs, no matter which model you use.

Whether you're solving problems, planning projects, or writing imaginative stories, these techniques help you move from asking questions to shaping thoughtful, high-quality responses. Here, prompting becomes more than a tool it becomes a skill you can grow with confidence.

1. Chain-of-Thought Prompts

Chain-of-thought (CoT) prompting helps the AI walk through a problem the same way a person would step by step so you get clearer, more reliable answers on tricky tasks. Instead of expecting the model to jump straight to a conclusion, you ask it to "think aloud" by prompting phrases like "Let's reason step by step" or "Show your working," which encourages the model to break a problem into smaller pieces, explain its assumptions, and connect the dots.

This approach is especially useful for beginners facing puzzles in math, ethics, or strategy because it reduces sudden, unexplained leaps and makes the model's reasoning easy to follow and critique. To use CoT effectively, give a short domain cue (for example, "As a math tutor" or "From a consequentialist perspective"), limit the chain's length when you need focus, and ask for a final concise summary at the end so you get both the working and a clear takeaway. Over time, reading and refining these step-by-step answers not only improves the results you receive but also helps you learn how to think through problems more systematically yourself.

Prompt :

1. Ethical Dilemma Dissector:

"As an ethicist, dissect this dilemma [e.g., 'self-driving car crash choice'] using chain-of-thought: Step 1: Identify stakeholders and harms; Step 2: Weigh utilitarian vs. deontological principles with pros/cons; Step 3: Propose hybrid resolution; Step 4: Reflect on biases. Limit to 300 words, balanced tone. Output: Numbered steps > Decision matrix table > Personal application question."

2. Math Mystery Mapper:

"Map solving [equation, e.g., '2x + 3 = 11'] via CoT for a student: Step 1: Isolate variable visually (e.g., 'Picture scales balancing'); Step 2: Algebraic moves with checks; Step 3: Verify with plug-in; Step 4: Extend to word problem. Encouraging voice, 200 words. Format: Step chain > Visual analogy > Practice variant."

3. Recipe Reasoning Refiner:

"Refine this recipe [paste ingredients/steps] with CoT: Step 1: Assess flavor balance (sweet/savory ratios); Step 2: Sequence for efficiency (prep/cook overlaps); Step 3: Adapt for dietary needs; Step 4: Predict pitfalls. Culinary tone. Output: Refined steps > Balance chart > Substitution swaps."

4. Business Bottleneck Breaker:

"Break a bottleneck [e.g., 'team workflow snag'] via CoT: Step 1: Map process flow; Step 2: Pinpoint friction (e.g., handoffs); Step 3: Brainstorm 3 fixes with trade-offs; Step 4: Prioritize by ROI. Strategic voice, 250 words. Format: Flow diagram text > Fix table > Implementation timeline."

5. Story Plot Polisher:

"Polish this plot outline [paste summary] with CoT: Step 1: Arc check (setup/rise/climax/fall/resolution); Step 2: Character motivation gaps; Step 3: Tension builders; Step 4: Ending twist feasibility. Narrative tone. Output: Revised outline > Gap bridges > Reader hook teaser."

6. Code Logic:

"Debug [code snippet, e.g., 'loop error'] via CoT: Step 1: Trace execution path; Step 2: Hypothesize bugs (e.g., index off); Step 3: Test isolates; Step 4: Refactor with guards. Programmer's voice, 220 words. Format: Trace log > Bug hypotheses > Patched code diff."

7. Travel Itinerary Thinker:

"Think through an itinerary for [trip, e.g., '3-day Tokyo']: Step 1: Prioritize must-sees by theme; Step 2: Logistics chain (transit/time zones); Step 3: Buffer for spontaneity; Step 4: Budget sanity check. Adventurous tone. Output: Day-by-day schedule > Theme map > Flex adjustments."

8. Fitness Goal Forecaster:

"Forecast a fitness plan [e.g., 'marathon prep'] with CoT: Step 1: Baseline assessment; Step 2: Progressive overload phases; Step 3: Recovery integrations; Step 4: Milestone metrics. Motivating voice. Format: Phase ladder > Metric dashboard > Plateau predictor."

9. Debate Defense Developer:

"Develop a debate stance on [topic, e.g., 'remote work pros/cons'] via CoT: Step 1: Core argument thesis; Step 2: Evidence stack (3 sources); Step 3: Counter rebuttals; Step 4: Closing persuasion. Rhetorical tone, 280 words. Output: Stance structure > Rebuttal table > Delivery tips."

10. Design Decision Decoder:

"Decode a design choice [e.g., 'app UI color scheme'] with CoT: Step 1: User persona needs; Step 2: Palette emotion mapping; Step 3: Accessibility audits; Step 4: A/B test rationale. Creative voice. Format: Persona profiles > Palette psych > Test protocol."

2. Multi-Agent Prompting

Multi-agent prompting lets you simulate a small team of AI “specialists” working together, making it much easier to tackle complex problems without feeling overwhelmed. Instead of relying on a single response, you create a virtual roundtable where each AI takes on a specific role such as an innovator who suggests bold ideas, a critic who spots flaws, or a strategist who brings everything together.

By giving each role clear instructions and setting simple rules for how they should interact (for example, “Three rounds of discussion, then agree on a final answer”), you guide them to debate, refine, and improve ideas just like a real brainstorming session. This method is perfect for beginners because it breaks down complicated tasks into manageable viewpoints and helps reveal insights you might not have considered.

Whether you're generating creative concepts, improving a project, or reviewing decisions from multiple angles, multi-agent prompting gives you a structured yet easy way to think more deeply without needing any prior expertise.

Prompt :

1. Innovation Council Convener:

"Convene a 3-agent council for [idea, e.g., 'eco-app concept']: Agent 1 (Innovator): Brainstorm 3 features; Agent 2 (Critic): Poke holes; Agent 3 (Integrator): Synthesize viable prototype. 3 rounds max, collaborative tone. Output: Round dialogues > Final pitch > Feasibility score (1-10)."

2. Marketing Mix Mediator:

"Mediate a multi-agent strategy for [campaign, e.g., 'product launch']: Agent 1 (Strategist): Target personas; Agent 2 (Copywriter): Messaging hooks; Agent 3 (Analyst): Channel ROI. Converge in summary. Professional voice, 300 words. Format: Agent inputs table > Mediated plan > KPI trackers."

3. Code Review Roundtable:

"Roundtable code review with 4 agents on [snippet, e.g., 'API endpoint']: Agent 1 (Security): Vulnerabilities; Agent 2 (Perf): Optimizations; Agent 3 (UX): Usability; Agent 4 (Doc): Clarity. Iterative fixes. Technical tone. Output: Review threads > Revised code > Best practice notes."

4. Story Swarm Simulator:

"Simulate a story swarm for [premise, e.g., 'time-travel romance']: Agent 1 (Plotter): Arc beats; Agent 2 (Character): Depth layers; Agent 3 (Twist): Surprises; Agent 4 (Editor): Pacing polish. Narrative convergence. Output: Swarm synopsis > Character arcs > Edit redline."

5. Budget Balancing Board:

"Board a budget debate for [project, e.g., '$10k startup seed']: Agent 1 (Thrifty): Cuts; Agent 2 (Bold): Investments; Agent 3 (Balancer): Compromises. Data-driven, 250 words. Format: Debate ledger > Balanced allocation pie (text) > Sensitivity analysis."

6. Recipe Remix Rendezvous:

"Rendezvous agents for recipe remix [base, e.g., 'vegan lasagna']: Agent 1 (Chef): Flavor fusions; Agent 2 (Nutritionist): Health tweaks; Agent 3 (Time-Saver): Simplifications. Tasty tone. Output: Agent contributions > Final recipe card > Pairing suggestions."

7. Fitness Forum Facilitator:

"Facilitate a fitness forum on [goal, e.g., 'beginner strength']: Agent 1 (Trainer): Routines; Agent 2 (Doc): Safety; Agent 3 (Motivator): Mindset; Agent 4 (Tracker): Progress. Supportive voice. Format: Forum posts > Consolidated plan > Milestone motivators."

8. Debate Duo Developer:

"Develop a debate duo for [issue, e.g., 'crypto regulation']: Agent 1 (Pro): Benefits; Agent 2 (Con): Risks; Converge on balanced policy. Nuanced tone, 280 words. Output: Duo exchanges > Policy hybrid > Implementation steps."

9. Design Jury Deliberator:

"Deliberate a design jury for [mockup, e.g., 'logo variant']: Agent 1 (Aesthetic): Visuals; Agent 2 (Brand): Alignment; Agent 3 (User): Appeal; Agent 4 (Tech): Scalability. Constructive voice. Format: Jury verdicts > Jury score > Iteration blueprint."

10. Travel Thinker:

"Thinker a travel troika for [itinerary, e.g., 'budget Europe']: Agent 1 (Explorer): Hidden gems; Agent 2 (Planner): Logistics; Agent 3 (Saver): Deals. Adventurous tone. Output: Troika talks > Optimized route > Surprise factor."

3. Recursive Prompting

Recursive prompting is a simple but powerful technique where you feed the AI's output back into the prompt to gradually improve the result almost like polishing a piece of writing or shaping a sculpture one refinement at a time. Instead of expecting a perfect answer in one shot, you guide the AI through small improvement cycles, each making the response clearer, sharper, and more aligned with what you want.

Beginners can use this easily by setting a limit for how many refinement loops they want (for example, 2 or 3 rounds) and defining a stopping rule such as "stop when the result feels coherent and complete." This method works especially well when you're trying to polish sentences, improve creative ideas, develop structured plans, or explore different versions of the same concept. It's a gentle, iterative way to get high-quality results without needing expert-level prompting skills.

Prompt :

1. Prose Polish Recycler:

"Recursively refine this draft [paste paragraph]: Cycle 1: Clarity scan (cut fluff); Cycle 2: Flow enhancement (transitions); Cycle 3: Voice amplification (tone tweaks). Stop at vivid coherence, 3 cycles max. Editorial tone. Output: Cycle evolutions > Final polish > Strength metrics."

2. Plan Precision Pumper:

"Pump a business plan [outline] recursively: Iteration 1: Gap hunt; Iteration 2: Risk buffer; Iteration 3: Scalability stretch. Converge on robust version. Strategic voice, 250 words per cycle. Format: Iteration logs > Enhanced plan > Delta summary."

3. Idea Incubator Loop:

"Loop an idea incubation for [seed, e.g., 'sustainable gadget']: Round 1: Expand facets; Round 2: Feasibility filter; Round 3: Innovation inject; Round 4: Market mate. Creative tone. Output: Loop branches > Matured concept > Prototype sketch."

4. Code Cleanse Cycle:

"Cycle a code cleanse on [snippet]: Pass 1: Syntax scrub; Pass 2: Efficiency edge; Pass 3: Readability refactor. Halt at optimal. Programmer's voice. Format: Pass diffs > Clean code > Test suite add."

5. Narrative Nest Builder:

"Build a narrative nest recursively from [prompt, e.g., 'detective noir opener']: Layer 1: Scene set; Layer 2: Clue drop; Layer 3: Twist tease; Layer 4: Cliff polish. Atmospheric tone, 4 layers. Output: Nested layers > Cohesive scene > Sequel seed."

6. Budget Bootstrap Bounce:

"Bounce a budget bootstrap [initial figures]: Recursion 1: Categorize spends; Recursion 2: Cut candidates; Recursion 3: Reinvest options. Balance at viable. Fiscal voice. Format: Bounce table > Bootstrapped ledger > Forecast flex."

7. Fitness Form Forge:

"Forge fitness form recursively [routine draft]: Cycle 1: Balance check; Cycle 2: Progression plot; Cycle 3: Recovery weave. Converge on sustainable. Motivating tone. Output: Cycle forms > Forged routine > Adherence anchors."

8. Debate Depth Digger:

"Digger debate depth on [thesis]: Recurse 1: Evidence excavate; Recurse 2: Counter carve; Recurse 3: Rebut reinforce. Depth at dialectical. Rhetorical voice, 200 words/cycle. Format: Dig levels > Deepened thesis > Dialogue sim."

9. Design Detail Driller:

"Driller design details from [sketch]: Loop 1: Element enumerate; Loop 2: Harmony hone; Loop 3: User usability. Drill to detailed. Creative tone. Output: Loop drills > Detailed render > User test tease."

10. Recipe Refine Reel:

"Reel a recipe refine [base]: Reel 1: Ingredient inspect; Reel 2: Step streamline; Reel 3: Taste test sim. Reel to ready. Culinary voice. Format: Reel rounds > Refined recipe > Flavor forecast."

4. Role-Stacking & Character Simulation

Role-stacking is an easy technique where you ask the AI to take on multiple personas at once so you can get richer, more layered responses. Instead of relying on a single perspective, you guide the AI through combined roles, like asking it to think first as a historian and then express the result as a poet to create responses that feel more nuanced and multidimensional. A related method, character simulation, asks the AI to act as if it's a person in a story or scenario, which makes conversations more immersive and often more empathetic. Beginners can start simply by stacking two roles or by asking the AI to "evolve" through stages.

For example, shifting from skeptic to supporter over the course of a dialogue. These techniques are especially useful for writing, creative brainstorming, role-play exercises, emotional exploration, or training simulations, because they add depth, personality, and realism without requiring any advanced skill.

Prompt :

1. Historian-Poet Hybrid:

"Stack roles as historian-poet for [event, e.g., 'fall of Rome']: Layer 1 (Historian): Factual chronicle; Layer 2 (Poet): Lyrical lament. Blend in 250 words, evocative tone. Output: Layered narrative > Poetic verse excerpt > Legacy lens."

2. Mentor-to-Muse:

"Morph from mentor to muse in advising [goal, e.g., 'career pivot']: Start structured (goals/steps), evolve inspirational (visions/ metaphors). Guiding voice, 300 words. Format: Morph arc > Actionable advice > Muse mantra."

3. Detective-Doctor Duo:

"Duo as detective-doctor on [mystery, e.g., 'symptom puzzle']: Detective probes clues; Doctor diagnoses ties. Converge on solution. Investigative tone. Output: Duo dialogue > Diagnosis diff > Prevention plot."

4. Chef-Critic Cascade:

"Cascade chef-critic for [dish review, e.g., 'fusion tacos']: Chef crafts praise; Critic constructs critique; Stack to elevated recipe. Flavorful voice. Format: Cascade comments > Stacked revision > Pairing poem."

5. Warrior-Wisdom Weaver:

“Weaver warrior-wisdom for [challenge, e.g., 'overcoming fear']: Warrior charges tactics; Wisdom weaves reflections. Epic tone, 220 words. Output: Woven tale > Tactical toolkit > Reflective ritual."

6. Journalist-Jester Jig:

"Jig journalist-jester on [news, e.g., 'tech breakthrough']: Journalist facts first; Jester jabs insights. Witty convergence. Output: Jig journal > Punchy insights > Satire sketch."

7. Explorer-Ecologist Echo:

"Echo explorer-ecologist for [journey, e.g., 'Amazon trek']: Explorer adventures; Ecologist echoes impacts. Wonder-filled voice. Format: Echo entries > Impact inventory > Conservation call."

8. Sculptor-Scholar Stack:

"Stack sculptor-scholar for [artifact, e.g., 'ancient vase']: Scholar deciphers history; Sculptor shapes modern meaning. Artistic tone, 280 words. Output: Stacked study > Symbolic sculpture > Exhibit envision."

9. Rebel-Reformer Reel:

"Reel rebel-reformer on [issue, e.g., 'corporate greed']: Rebel rants roots; Reformer reels remedies. Passionate voice. Format: Reel rants > Reform roadmap > Rally rhyme."

10. Dreamer-Detailer:

"Drift dreamer-detailer for [vision, e.g., 'utopian city']: Dreamer drifts ideals; Detailer docks designs. Visionary tone. Output: Drift dialogue > Detailed blueprint > Dream diary prompt."

5. Meta-Prompts (Prompts that Improve Prompts)

Meta-prompts are prompts about prompts, self-reflective engines that debug, enhance, or generate better ones, cutting iteration time by 50% (PromptBase 2025). Beginners use them as "prompt doctors": Feed a weak query, get a fortified version; constrain to specificity for targeted upgrades, revolutionizing your prompting meta-game.

Prompt :

1. Prompt Polisher Prime:

"Prime a prompt polish for [raw prompt, e.g., 'explain AI']: Audit clarity/gaps, suggest ICCEF upgrades (e.g., add constraints), output v2 with rationale. Meta tone, 150 words. Output: Audit table > Polished prompt > Efficacy boost estimate."

2. Bias Buster Builder:

"Build a bias-buster meta for [query, e.g., 'job interview tips']: Scan for assumptions, inject diverse lenses, refine inclusive version. Equitable voice. Format: Bias flags > Balanced build > Test query."

3. Complexity Compressor:

"Compress complexity in [overlong prompt]: Trim fluff, chain logic, cap at 100 words while retaining depth. Efficient tone. Output: Compression log > Sleek version > Fidelity check."

4. Role Refiner Recycler:

"Recycler role refiner for [persona prompt, e.g., 'as CEO']: Enhance with traits/motivations, add conflict hooks, v2 with examples. Immersive voice. Format: Trait tree > Refined role > Simulation snippet."

5. Output Optimizer Oracle:

"Oracle output optimizer for [prompt goal, e.g., 'business plan']: Prescribe format tweaks (e.g., tables for SWOT), constrain for scannability. Strategic tone, 200 words. Output: Optimization oracle > Tuned prompt > Sample output preview."

6. Ambiguity Annihilator:

"Annihilate ambiguity in [vague prompt, e.g., 'help with writing']: Probe intents, add exemplars/constraints, fortified fork. Clarifying voice. Format: Ambiguity audit > Annihilated alt > Branch choices."

7. Engagement Enhancer Engine:

"Engine an engagement enhancer for [content prompt, e.g., 'social post']: Infuse hooks/CTAs, persona-tune, v2 with virality cues. Dynamic tone. Output: Enhancer metrics > Amped prompt > Engagement forecast."

8. Scalability Scalpel:

"Scalpel scalability into [niche prompt, e.g., 'local marketing']: Broaden for global, add variables, refined for adaptability. Expansive voice. Format: Scalpel slices > Scaled prompt > Adaptation playbook."

9. Creativity Catalyst Crafter:

"Crafter a creativity catalyst for [stale prompt, e.g., 'describe a tree']: Inject wild cards (e.g., 'as alien flora'), iterate sparks, v2 burst. Inventive tone. Output: Catalyst charges > Catalyzed prompt > Spark storm ideas."

10. Validation Vault Keeper:

"Keeper a validation vault for [prompt output rubric]: Generate self-check questions, score criteria, meta-refine. Rigorous voice. Format: Vault questions > Score sheet > Refinement loop."

6. Long-Context Prompting (Gemini 1.5 Pro Max Style)

Long-context prompting is a technique that takes advantage of modern AI models' ability to remember and work with extremely large amounts of information at once. Instead of giving the AI short snippets, you can feed it long documents, detailed stories, or multiple sources, and the model can connect everything into one coherent output. This makes it incredibly useful for tasks like summarizing long reports, building multi-chapter narratives, analyzing historical timelines, or synthesizing research. For beginners, the easiest way to use long-context prompting is to start with a clear summary, break your material into manageable chunks, and remind the AI to "recall earlier sections" when needed. Adding simple constraints like asking it to stay on topic or follow a specific structure helps keep the output focused. With the right setup, long-context prompting transforms large collections of information into clear, meaningful, and beautifully connected results.

Prompt :

1. Document Digest Weaver:

"Weave a digest from [long doc excerpts, e.g., '10-page report']: Chunk into themes, cross-reference (e.g., 'Link sec 2 to 7'), synthesize executive brief. Analytical tone, 400 words. Output: Theme tapestry > Key cross-links > Action agenda."

2. Saga Seed Sustainer:

"Sustain a saga from [prior chapters summary + new prompt, e.g., 'hero's return']: Recall arcs/characters, extend 500 words with consistency checks. Epic voice. Format: Recall recap > Sustained scene > Arc alignment."

3. Legal Lore Layerer:

"Layer legal analysis on [contract chunks]: Reference clauses across sections, flag inconsistencies, propose amendments. Precise tone. Output: Clause layers > Inconsistency map > Amendment docket."

4. Research Review Recycler:

"Recycler a research review from [paper abstracts + notes]: Synthesize gaps/trends, cite interconnections, forward agenda. Scholarly voice, 350 words. Format: Review recycle > Gap graph > Horizon hints."

5. Novel Nest Nurturer:

"Nurture a novel nest from [character bios + plot beats]: Recall motivations, nest new chapter with tension ties. Immersive tone. Output: Nest nurture > Chapter weave > Foreshadow file."

6. Policy Projector:

"Project policy impacts from [historical precedents + current bill]: Prism parallels, project 3 scenarios with recalls. Forward-thinking voice. Format: Prism projections > Scenario spectra > Policy pivot points."

7. Code Curator:

"Curator a code corpus from [module summaries + new feature]: Recall dependencies, curate integration with tests. Technical tone, 300 words. Output: Corpus curate > Integration code > Dependency diagram."

8. Therapy Thread Tracer:

"Tracer therapy threads from [session transcripts summary]: Recall patterns/emotions, trace growth arc, suggest next session. Empathetic voice. Format: Thread traces > Growth graph > Session seed."

9. Market Memo Mapper:

"Mapper market memos from [trend reports + data dumps]: Map evolutions with cross-era recalls, memo 2026 forecast. Strategic tone. Output: Memo map > Evolution edges > Forecast frame."

10. Mythos Memory Minder:

"Minder a mythos memory from [lore entries + new tale]: Recall pantheon ties, mind expanded myth with motifs. Mythic voice, 450 words. Format: Memory minder > Myth expansion > Motif mosaic."

Specialized Prompt Packs

Specialized prompt packs are like ready-made toolkits designed for specific types of work, making it easier for beginners to get strong results without feeling overwhelmed. Instead of using the same generic prompts for everything, these packs give developers, designers, writers, students, startups, and creators focused guidance that matches the tasks they actually do. Studies show that role-specific prompts can improve efficiency by more than 40%, which is why they're so helpful when you want clear, reliable outcomes. In this chapter, each prompt pack is crafted to be practical and beginner-friendly. They use simple but powerful techniques like adding the right vocabulary for each profession, refining results step-by-step, and using helpful personas to deepen understanding. All prompts follows:

1. Clarity
2. Context
3. Constraints
4. Examples
5. Format

So you can use them instantly. Just add your details, review what the AI gives you, and adjust as needed. No matter which AI model you prefer, these prompts are designed to support your craft, whether you're building an app, creating content, studying, or writing stories. These packs aren't just prompts, they're starting points that help you create faster, better, and with more confidence.

1. Prompt Pack for Developers

Developers work in a fast-paced digital environment where building and fixing code can feel both exciting and challenging. With modern AI tools now helping reduce debugging time by more than a third, beginners have a real advantage when they know how to guide these tools effectively. This prompt pack is designed to support new developers by giving them clear, practical ways to use AI for coding tasks. It combines step-by-step reasoning for clearer logic, simple role-based prompts for better feedback, and helpful constraints to keep code clean and error-free. Whether you're writing your first script, troubleshooting bugs, or planning an API, these prompts make the process easier, more organized, and far less overwhelming.

Prompt :

1. API Blueprint Builder:

"As a senior API architect, blueprint an endpoint for [function, e.g., 'user auth']: Chain CoT, Step 1: Define schema (inputs/outputs); Step 2: Security layers (JWT/OAuth); Step 3: Error handling with codes; Step 4: Scalability notes. Output: Swagger-like YAML snippet > Test curl example > Edge case table."

2. Bug Hunt Handler:

"Hunt bugs as a debug duo (junior + vet) on [code snippet]: Junior traces flow; Vet hypothesizes fixes; Converge on patch. Constrain to Python/JS, 200 words. Format: Duo dialogue > Diff patch > Unit test stubs."

3. Refactor Ritual Refiner:

"Refine a refactor ritual for [legacy code, e.g., 'monolith function']: Recurse 3x:1: Modularize; 2: Optimize loops; 3: Doc inline. Clean code principles. Output: Iteration evos > Refactored module > Perf delta estimate."

4. Database Design Driller:

"Drill a DB design for [app, e.g., 'e-com inventory']: Stack roles, DBA schemas, Query optimizer indexes, Security auditor constraints. ER diagram text. Format: Schema table > Query samples > Normalization score."

5. Frontend Flux Forecaster:

"Forecast frontend flux for [feature, e.g., 'dark mode toggle']: CoT components (state/hooks), accessibility checks, perf audits. React/ Vue agnostic. Output: Component tree > Toggle logic > Lighthouse sim."

6. DevOps Deployment Dreamer:

"Dream a DevOps pipeline for [deploy, e.g., 'CI/CD to AWS']: Agents collaborate, Builder scripts, Tester gates, Monitorer alerts. YAML focus. Format: Pipeline stages > Agent inputs > Rollback ritual."

7. Algo Ascent Advisor:

"Advise an algo ascent for [problem, e.g., 'sort large datasets']: CoT Big O, pseudocode to impl, trade-offs. Beginner-friendly. Output: Asymptote analysis > Coded solution > Benchmark bash."

8. Testing Throne Tactician:

"Tactician testing throne for [module, e.g., 'login form']: Meta-prompt for test cases (unit/e2e), coverage goals, mocks. Jest/ Cypress vibe. Format: Test suite outline > Coverage matrix > Flaky fixers."

9. Microservice Map Maker:

"Make a microservice map for [system, e.g., 'chat app']: Recursive boundaries, comms (gRPC/REST), orchestration. Output: Service graph ASCII > API contracts > Fault tolerance flows."

10. Code Review Ritualizer:

"Ritualize a code review for [PR description]: Multi-agent, Reviewer comments, Author responses, Merger merges. GitHub style. Format: Review threads > Merged decisions > Best practice bible."

2. Prompt Pack for Designers

Designers bring ideas to life by shaping visuals, layouts, and identities that feel both beautiful and practical. With modern AI tools boosting creative output by nearly half, beginners now have powerful support to explore ideas more confidently. This prompt pack helps new designers start strong by offering simple ways to guide AI with visual cues, ask for multiple variations, and even simulate professional design critiques. You can begin with broad concepts like asking for styles inspired by well-known movements and then refine them through repeated improvements or feedback-driven adjustments. Whether you're sketching early wireframes or polishing a final prototype, these prompts help streamline your creative process and make design feel more approachable, structured, and enjoyable.

Prompts :

1. Wireframe Whisperer:

"Whisper a wireframe for [UI, e.g., 'dashboard overview']: CoT user flows (entry > action > exit), low-fi elements, responsive breakpoints. Sketch text. Output: Flow diagram > Element inventory > Hi-fi evolution prompt."

2. Color Cosmos Curator:

"Curate a color cosmos for [brand, e.g., 'tech startup']: Stack palettes Psych evoker, Access auditor, Trend tracker. 5 hues max. Format: Swatch spectrum > Harmony hexes > Mood mapping."

3. Icon Idea Incubator:

"Incubate icons recursively for [concept, e.g., 'share button']: Layer 1: Sketch variants; Layer 2: Simplify lines; Layer 3: Test scalability. SVG hints. Output: Iteration icons > Vector desc > App integration."

4. Typography Teacher:

"Teach a typography tango for [project, e.g., 'e-book layout']: Agents dance, Pairer fonts, Kerner spacing, Hierarcher scales. Serif/sans mix. Format: Pair playbook > Scale ladder > Readability rubric."

5. Mood Board Mosaic Maker:

"Make a mood board mosaic for [theme, e.g., 'cyberpunk UI']: Multi-agent harvest Visualizer textures, Curator refs, Synthesizer story. Image prompt ready. Output: Mosaic elements > Narrative thread > Collage comp."

6. Prototyping Path Paver:

"Pave a prototyping path for [feature, e.g., 'onboarding flow']: CoT screens (3-5), interactions (swipes/taps), feedback loops. Figma-like. Format: Screen sequence > Micro-anim desc > User test script."

7. Logo Lore Layerer:

"Layer logo lore for [brand, e.g., 'eco-cafe']: Recursive refine 1: Symbol brainstorm; 2: Type fuse; 3: Versatility vet. Monochrome start. Output: Layer logs > Logo lockup > Merch mock ideas."

8. UX Empathy Engine:

"Engine UX empathy for [persona, e.g., 'busy parent shopper']: Role-stack journey Empath pains, Mapper solutions, Validator validations. Pain-point focus. Format: Journey map > Solution sketches > A/B empathy test."

9. Illustration Impulse Igniter:

"Ignite illustration impulses for [scene, e.g., 'futuristic market']: CoT composition (rule of thirds), style refs (e.g., Syd Mead), detail deltas. Prompt for Midjourney. Output: Comp canvas > Style stack > Variant visions."

10. Brand Bible Builder:

"Build a brand bible recursively from [essentials, e.g., 'voice guidelines']: Cycle 1: Visual vault; Cycle 2: Tone tenets; Cycle 3: Usage universe. Comprehensive cap. Format: Bible sections > Usage dos/don'ts > Audit checklist."

3. Prompt Pack for Writers

Writers often start with just a spark of an idea and work to shape it into a meaningful story, article, or message. With today's AI tools helping people write more while still keeping their unique voice, beginners can develop their skills faster and with more confidence. This prompt pack gives new writers a simple, supportive framework to build stronger plots, develop deeper characters, and refine their prose step by step. You'll learn how to guide AI through clear reasoning for plot development, simulate character behavior to add realism, and polish drafts through gentle iterative improvements. Whether you're writing fiction, essays, or content for work, these prompts help you break through blocks, stay organized, and bring your ideas to life in a smoother, more enjoyable way.

Prompt :

1. Plot Pyramid Pusher:

"Push a plot pyramid for [genre, e.g., 'sci-fi thriller']: CoT acts (inciting > rising > climax), twists per tier, character catalysts. 500-word outline. Output: Pyramid prose > Twist table > Pacing pulse."

2. Character Crafter:

"Crafter a character crucible [archetype, e.g., 'flawed hero']: Simulate arc, Backstory burn, Conflict forge, Growth quench. Internal monologue heavy. Format: Crucible stages > Monologue mosaic > Arc mirror question."

3. Dialogue Dynamo Developer:

"Develop dialogue dynamo for [scene, e.g., 'tense negotiation']: Multi-agent voices (speaker quirks), subtext stacks, rhythm recurs. 300 words. Output: Dynamo exchanges > Subtext subtitles > Ear-test edit."

4. World Whisper Weaver:

"Weave world whispers for [setting, e.g., 'underwater dystopia']: Recursive layers: 1: Sensory skin; 2: Societal sinews; 3: Magic mechanics. Immersive tone. Format: Layer loom > Whisper vignette > Map murmur."

5. Prose Polish Pendulum:

"Pendulum prose polish on [draft excerpt]: Meta-swing: 1: Clarity chop; 2: Rhythm swing; 3: Imagery ignite. Literary voice, 250 words. Output: Swing scores > Polished passage > Voice vibe check."

6. Flash Fiction:

"Forge flash fiction from [prompt, e.g., 'last library on Earth']: CoT constraint (500 words, twist end), theme threads, echo endings. Compact craft. Format: Forge beats > Fiction flash > Echo extensions."

7. Poem Persona Painter:

"Painter a poem persona for [muse, e.g., 'forgotten inventor']: Role-stack forms (sonnet stanza, free verse flow), metaphor mines. Poetic pulse. Output: Persona palette > Poem portrait > Recite rhythm."

8. Non-Fic Narrative Nudger:

"Nudger non-fic narrative for [topic, e.g., 'AI's rise']: Agents nudge, Researcher facts, Storyteller arcs, Editor ethics. 400 words. Format: Nudge notes > Narrative nest > Fact-file footer."

9. Revision Ritual Reframer:

"Reframer revision ritual for [manuscript section]: Recursive rites: 1: Plot probe; 2: Prose prune; 3: Pace pulse. Writer's workshop vibe. Output: Ritual rounds > Reframed revision > Beta reader bait."

10. Query Quest:

"Quiller a query quest for [pitch, e.g., 'debut novel synopsis']: CoT hook (comp titles), stakes stack, agent allure. Professional poise, 200 words. Output: Quest query > Comp comps > Submission spell."

4. Prompt Pack for Students

Students often juggle classes, notes, deadlines, and expectations, all while trying to truly understand what they're learning. With AI study tools now helping many learners stay organized and improve performance, beginners can use the right prompts to make studying clearer and less overwhelming. This prompt pack is designed to support students step by step: breaking down difficult topics into simple explanations, turning notes into quizzes for active recall, and simulating helpful tutor-style guidance when clarity is needed. These prompts help build stronger study habits, make homework easier to manage, and turn confusion into confidence. Whether preparing for exams, summarizing chapters, or reviewing complex ideas, students can use these tools to learn smarter, not harder.

Prompt :

1. Concept Cascade Clarifier:

"Clarifier a concept cascade for [subject, e.g., 'photosynthesis cycle']: CoT steps (inputs > processes > outputs), analogies anchor, quiz cap. Student-friendly, 250 words. Output: Cascade chain > Analogy album > Quick-quiz quartet."

2. Essay Engine Emulator:

"Emulator an essay engine for [thesis, e.g., 'social media's impact']: Stack structure, Outliner intro, Arguer body, Synthesizer concl. APA/MLA cue. Format: Engine outline > Draft dynamo > Rubric rehearsal."

3. Flashcard Facilitator:

"Facilitator flashcard forge for [terms, e.g., 'psychology biases']: Recursive refine: 1: Def draft; 2: Example etch; 3: Mnemonic mint. Spaced repetition ready. Output: Forge deck > Mnemonic map > Review rhythm."

4. History Horizon Helper:

"Helper a history horizon for [era, e.g., 'Industrial Revolution']: Multi-agent timeline, Eventer dates, Impact agent, Legacy linker. Visual vignettes. Format: Horizon hurdles > Impact icons > Debate diver."

5. Math Maze Mapper:

"Mapper a math maze for [problem, e.g., 'quadratic solver']: CoT path (factor > graph > verify), visual vars, trap tips. Encouraging tone. Output: Maze map > Solved shortcuts > Practice puzzle."

6. Lit Layer Lifter:

"Lifter lit layers for [text, e.g., 'Great Gatsby quotes']: Agents lift, Analyzer symbols, Connector contexts, Critic critiques. Thematic ties. Format: Layer lifts > Quote quilt > Essay ember."

7. Study Sprint Scheduler:

"Scheduler a study sprint for [exam, e.g., 'midterm bio']: Recursive rounds: 1: Topic triage; 2: Resource rally; 3: Review rally. Pomodoro pulse. Output: Sprint schedule > Resource roster > Burnout buffer."

8. Sci Simulacrum Simulator:

"Simulator a sci simulacrum for [experiment, e.g., 'acid-base reaction']: CoT hypothesis > method > results > concl, virtual vars. Lab-lite voice. Format: Sim steps > Result recap > Extension expo."

9. Lang Learner:

"Learner lang lore for [phrase, e.g., 'French idioms']: Role-stack cultural context, usage unpacks, convo crafts. Immersive immersion. Output: Lore layers > Idiom idioms > Chat challenge."

10. Thesis Thread Thinker:

"Thinker a thesis thread for [research, e.g., 'climate policy effects']: Meta-thread, Question quest, Source sift, Argue arc. Academic arc. Format: Thread thoughts > Source synthesis > Peer polish prompt."

5. Prompt Pack for Startups

Startups move fast, and early founders often juggle uncertainty, big ideas, and limited resources all at once. AI can make this journey easier by helping beginners think more clearly, plan more strategically, and adapt more quickly when things change. This prompt pack gives new founders practical tools to refine ideas, map out simple roadmaps, and run through pitch-style simulations without needing a full team. By breaking decisions into step-by-step reasoning, exploring different perspectives, and refining plans through small iterative improvements, these prompts help transform rough concepts into focused, workable strategies.

Whether you're shaping your first MVP, testing assumptions, or preparing to present your startup vision, this pack provides a supportive starting point for building with confidence and direction.

Prompts :

1. Pitch Deck Polisher:

"Polisher a pitch deck for [idea, e.g., 'AI meal planner']: CoT slides (problem > sol > market > traction), visual vibes, investor intrigue. 10-slide cap. Output: Deck desc > Slide stack > Q&A quiver."

2. MVP Map Maker:

"Maker an MVP map for [product, e.g., 'chatbot tool']: Multi-agent minimal, Builder features, Tester viability, Seller value. Lean launch. Format: Map milestones > Feature funnel > Beta bait."

3. Funding Forecast Facilitator:

"Facilitator funding forecast [stage, e.g., 'seed round']: Recursive raise: 1: Deck draft; 2: Ask anchor; 3: Term tweak. Fiscal flair. Output: Forecast flows > Ask arsenal > VC vibe check."

4. Customer Canvas Curator:

"Curator a customer canvas for [persona, e.g., 'solo founder']: Stack empathy, Pain painter, Gain gatherer, Journey jotter. Lean canvas lite. Format: Canvas quadrants > Persona portrait > Interview ignite."

5. Path Paver:

"Paver a pivot path from [stagnant stat, e.g., 'low retention']: CoT causes (data dive), options orbit, test trajectory. Agile arc. Output: Path paves > Option odds > Metric monitor."

6. Team Talent Tactician:

"Tactician team talent for [roles, e.g., 'early hires']: Agents assess, Founder fits, Skill scanner, Culture curator. Growth guild. Format: Talent table > Fit forecast > Onboard oracle."

7. Growth Hack Generator:

"Generator growth hacks for [channel, e.g., 'LinkedIn lead gen']: Recursive riffs: 1: Hook hypothesize; 2: Test tweak; 3: Scale spike. Viral vibe. Output: Hack hierarchy > Test template > ROI radar."

8. Risk Radar Refiner:

"Refiner risk radar for [venture, e.g., 'fintech app']: Multi-agent scan, Market mapper, Legal lurker, Tech trapper. Vigilant voice. Format: Radar rings > Risk roster > Mitigation map."

9. Brand Beacon Builder:

"Builder a brand beacon [essence, e.g., 'disruptive edtech']: CoT core (values > voice > visuals), beacon blasts. Magnetic tone. Output: Beacon blueprint > Voice vault > Launch lighthouse."

10. Exit Echo Envisioner:

"Envisioner an exit echo [horizon, e.g., '5-year acquisition']: Recursive roads: 1: Value vault; 2: Buyer brainstorm; 3: Deal dance. Visionary voice. Format: Echo evos > Road runners > Legacy ledger."

6. Prompt Pack for Social Media Creators

Social media creators live at the intersection of creativity and constant change, where every post is a chance to connect, inspire, or go viral. For beginners, this world can feel overwhelming, algorithms shift, trends move fast, and finding your voice takes practice. This prompt pack is designed to make that journey easier by helping you generate strong ideas, craft engaging hooks, and understand what keeps audiences watching. Using simple step-by-step reasoning, trend exploration, and gentle refinement loops, these prompts guide you from rough concepts to polished, platform-ready content. Whether you're building a personal brand, launching a creative page, or simply wanting your posts to resonate more consistently, this pack gives you the tools to create confidently and grow your presence with clarity.

Prompt :

1. Content Calendar:

"Conjurer a content calendar for [niche, e.g., 'travel hacks']: CoT themes (evergreen > timely), post pillars, engagement echoes. 30-day span. Output: Calendar grid > Pillar playbook > Trend tie-ins."

2. Reel Refiner:

"Refiner reel rhythm for [idea, e.g., 'morning routine']: Multi-agent montage, Hook harvester, Beat builder, CTA closer. 15-sec script. Format: Rhythm reels > Beat breakdown > Duet dynamo."

3. Caption Craft Catalyst:

"Catalyst caption craft [visual, e.g., 'sunset snap']: Recursive riffs: 1: Hook hum; 2: Story stitch; 3: Call cascade. Emoji essence. Output: Craft cycles > Caption comp > Hashtag harvest."

4. Trend Troika Tracker:

"Tracker a trend troika [viral, e.g., 'GRWM challenge']: Agents twist—Adapter adapts, Amplifier amps, Authenticator aligns. Fresh fusion. Format: Troika twists > Trend transcript > Remix roster."

5. Collab Compass Curator:

"Curator a collab compass for [partner, e.g., 'fitness influencer']: CoT synergies (shared > unique), pitch pulses, co-content cues. Mutual muse. Output: Compass coords > Pitch prose > Content co-op."

6. Meme Meta-Maker:

"Maker a meme meta for [mood, e.g., 'Monday blues']: Meta-morph templates, caption quips, share sparks. Witty warp. Format: Meta molds > Quip queue > Viral vector."

7. Story Sequence Spinner:

"Spinner a story sequence [arc, e.g., 'day in life']: Recursive reveals:1: Tease tap; 2: Build buzz; 3: Close cliff. Interactive ink. Output: Sequence spins > Sticker stack > Poll pulse."

8. Hashtag Horizon Hunter:

"Hunter a hashtag horizon [campaign, e.g., '#EcoWins']: CoT relevance (reach > resonance), combo chains, track trends. Discover dynamo. Format: Horizon hunt > Combo cascades > Track tally."

9. Feedback Facilitator:

"Facilitator feedback forge from [post analytics]: Agents audit, Engager echoes, Optimizor ops, Innovator ignites. Growth guild. Output: Forge findings > Audit arcs > Next nexus."

10. Viral Vision Voyager:

"Voyager a viral vision [concept, e.g., 'ASMR unboxing']: Multi-agent voyage, Visualizer vibes, Sound scaper, Share shaman. Enchanting echo. Format: Vision voyage > Element elixir > Algorithm align."

Resources

In the world of AI-powered creativity and productivity, the right tools can make your workflow smoother, faster, and far more enjoyable, especially if you're just getting started. Instead of thinking of tools and extensions as optional add-ons, this chapter treats them as helpful companions that support your ideas and turn them into real results. Here, you'll find a beginner-friendly guide to the most useful resources across different categories: browser extensions that help you capture ideas instantly, code editors that make scripting easier, AI platforms that work with text, images, audio, and video, productivity apps that organize your work, collaboration tools that make teamwork seamless, and even experimental tools that let you explore the cutting edge. For each tool, you'll understand not only what it does, but why it matters, how it pairs with prompting techniques like step-by-step reasoning or role-based thinking, and how it can speed up your process.

You'll also get clear details on key features, smart integration tips, common beginner mistakes to avoid, and simple pro-level tricks to help you work more efficiently. Rather than overwhelming you with a long list, this chapter helps you choose tools thoughtfully: try one at a time, test it with a prompt from earlier chapters, see if it improves your flow, and adjust as needed. The goal is to empower you with tools that truly support your creativity, making your experience with AI more intuitive, productive, and rewarding.

Recommended Tools & Extensions

1. Browser Extensions for Prompting & Ideation

Browser extensions are small but powerful tools that can instantly improve the way you work online, especially if you're new to prompt engineering. Think of them as lightweight helpers that quietly sit in your browser and make everyday tasks smoother whether you're saving ideas, generating quick drafts, analyzing images, or pulling information from a page without switching tools. With thousands of extensions available today, the key is to choose ones that genuinely support your workflow instead of overwhelming you with features you don't need.

The best extensions help you write clearer prompts, organize your thoughts, and capture inspiration the moment it appears on your screen. It's important to pay attention to privacy and permissions, since some extensions collect more data than necessary

1. GrammarlyGO

GrammarlyGO is an upgraded version of the classic Grammarly tool, expanding from basic proofreading into a helpful generative writing assistant. Instead of just catching spelling mistakes, it now helps beginners grow their ideas by suggesting clearer prompts, expanding complex thoughts, and even helping you frame chain-of-thought questions, for example, turning a simple ethical dilemma into a guided reasoning prompt. Its most helpful features include a tone detector that adjusts your writing style, a built-in plagiarism scanner for safety, and a prompt-rephrasing tool that makes your requests clearer and more effective.

It works directly inside places like Google Docs and Gmail, offering real-time suggestions as you type, which makes it perfect for beginners who want guidance without leaving their workflow. While it's extremely accurate, around 95% when dealing with subtle meaning, the free plan does limit the number of generative actions you can use each day (about 100). Still, it's one of the easiest tools to start with if you want smoother writing and better-structured prompts without feeling overwhelmed.

Aspect	Details
Beginner Pitfall	Ignoring tone mismatches in role-play.
Pro Hack	Use "Regenerate with [technique]" for meta-refine.

2. TabAI Summarizer

TabAI Summarizer is a free tool that works on all major browsers, and it's designed to help you turn messy research sessions into clear, usable insights. Instead of juggling multiple tabs, you can open the TabAI sidebar and instantly condense everything you're reading into simple summaries or even prompt-ready material. It can generate TL;DR overviews, create helpful keyword clouds, and export your extracted information as JSON if you want to organize or reuse it later.

One of its biggest strengths is batch processing being able to summarize several tabs at once can save you hours. The only downside is that it may occasionally misinterpret dense or highly technical pages, but switching on its "Fact-check mode" helps reduce those errors and keeps the output more accurate.

Aspect	Details
Beginner Pitfall	Summarizing without verification, cross with sources.
Pro Hack	Use for long-context: "Feed this tab synth to Gemini 1.5."

2. Code Generation Extensions for Prompt-Driven Coding

Code-generation extensions are some of the most helpful tools you can add to your IDE, especially if you're a beginner. They allow you to turn plain-language instructions into real, working code, which makes them perfect for quick prototypes, whether you're experimenting with a small Three.js scene or trying out one of the developer prompt packs later in the book.

The VS Code marketplace now has more than 20,000 AI extensions (as of 2025), so the key is to choose the ones that help you think through code step-by-step and improve your drafts with cleaner structure and smarter refactoring. However, keep in mind that AI-generated code can sometimes be incorrect or "hallucinated," so always test it in a safe environment like a sandbox. For even better reliability, pair these tools with built-in linters or formatters, this alone can help you catch up to 90% of common errors before running your program.

1. Github Copilot

GitHub Copilot (Free tier) is one of the most popular AI coding assistants because it can turn your natural-language prompts into real code snippets right inside your editor. It works inline, meaning you can type something like "Convert this step-by-step explanation into JavaScript" and Copilot will generate a clean, ready-to-use version for you. It also includes a built-in chat assistant that can explain code, help you understand errors, and guide you through debugging. Copilot's autocomplete suggestions appear as you type, and you can accept them with a simple tap, making your workflow noticeably smoother.

For many beginners, one of the biggest advantages is its ability to fill in up to 70% of common coding patterns automatically. The only limitation is that the free plan allows around 2,000 generated lines per month, while the Pro plan removes that cap and unlocks more advanced features. Overall, it's an excellent tool for learning, practicing, and speeding up everyday coding.

Aspect	Details
Beginner Pitfall	Accepting untested suggestions, run lint first.
Pro Hack	Chat for multi-agent: "Simulate dev review on this."

2. Cursor AI

Cursor AI (Free tier; VS Code fork) is a specialized, AI-powered coding editor built for people who want to write code through prompts as easily as typing plain English. Instead of just suggesting small snippets, Cursor can generate entire files or major refactors based on a single instruction, such as asking it to "rebuild this feature using a cleaner structure" or "turn this idea into a full project scaffold."

It includes a sidebar chat where you can discuss your code, ask questions, or request improvements, and its diff preview feature lets you review every change before applying it. You can apply changes instantly using a simple shortcut (Cmd+K), which makes the workflow fast and intuitive even for beginners.

Aspect	Details
Beginner Pitfall	Structure as "Step-by-step [task]."
Pro Hack	Use for multi-agent: "Simulate dev team on [this] snippet."

3. Replit Ghostwriter

This cloud-based IDE comes with Ghostwriter AI built directly into the editor, making it perfect for beginners who want to collaborate through prompts instead of complex setups. You can simply type an instruction like "review this canvas code using multiple AI agents" and Ghostwriter helps refine, debug, or generate new code instantly.

Because it's fully online, there's no installation or configuration required, and you can work with others in real time, making it great for team projects or learning environments. It also offers live deployment previews so you can instantly see how your code behaves, along with a built-in prompt history that lets you revisit and reuse past instructions. You can trigger the AI anytime with the simple command /ai followed by "Generate from Prompt."

The only downside is that everything depends on having a stable internet connection, but for most users who prefer simplicity and effortless setup, this cloud IDE is one of the easiest ways to start coding with AI assistance.

Aspect	**Details**
Beginner Pitfall	Offline gaps, cache prompts locally.
Pro Hack	Enable Replit sharing to collaborate on specific section

3. Free, Authoritative Guides That Teach Real Skills

People often say mastering AI is difficult, but the truth is that it becomes simple when you learn from the right sources. What slows most people down is not the complexity of AI, it's the lack of clarity about where to begin, what to study, and which frameworks truly matter. To cut through the noise, I compiled thirteen completely free, high-quality resources that teach prompting, structured workflows, and practical AI skills in a deep, actionable way. Each resource comes directly from official teams, trusted researchers, or highly credible educators, making this list one of the most reliable starting points for anyone who wants to become genuinely skilled at prompting.

1. OpenAI Academy: The practical prompt training ground

OpenAI Academy is the most practical, hands-on place to learn real prompt design from the team that builds ChatGPT. Unlike scattered tutorials online, these lessons come straight from engineers and product teams who develop the models themselves. The Academy teaches you foundational patterns such as structured prompting, system messages, role-based templates, and multi-step workflows. You also learn how to refine prompts through constraints, formatting, tone instructions, and iterative improvement. If you are new to AI, or even if you are already building with it, this resource gives you the most authentic, production-grade training available anywhere.

2. Google Gemini Prompting Guide

Google's Gemini Prompting Guide is a precise, context-driven manual created to help you craft prompts that work brilliantly with Gemini and Workspace tools. The guide explains how to embed contextual signals such as files from Docs, Gmail, Sheets, and Drive to dramatically improve response quality. It teaches you to break larger workflows into sequential tasks, structure prompts for multimodal reasoning, and shape the model's output using targeted constraints. Anyone using Google Workspace or Gemini for work will find this guide invaluable, especially because it demonstrates how prompt design changes when your data lives inside an enterprise ecosystem.

3. Anthropic Academy (Claude Learning Hub)

Anthropic's Academy is the official home for learning how to work effectively with Claude, particularly if you want accuracy, reasoning, and safety-conscious prompting. The platform offers clear principles for writing instructions that Claude follows consistently, as well as guidance on building apps or workflows that rely on Claude's structured thinking. It covers the importance of guardrails, prompt scaffolding, system instructions, and role clarity. If you're a developer, researcher, or professional using Claude, this guide teaches the reasoning-first approach that Claude excels at, making your outputs significantly more stable and trustworthy.

4. Learn Prompting ("How to Prompt")

Learn Prompting is one of the most comprehensive, research-backed courses available for free. It covers everything from foundational concepts to advanced prompting techniques, including chain-of-thought prompting, structured templates, few-shot prompting, multimodal techniques, and evaluation methods. What makes it exceptional is the progression: each module builds on the last, with exercises that push you to compare results, analyze differences, and build your own prompt patterns. This resource is perfect for learners who want academic-level depth without the overwhelming jargon.

5. Nano Banana Prompting Guide

Nano Banana (and its advanced version, Nano Banana Pro) is Google's official guide to image generation with Gemini. It shows how to control the model using cinematic instructions, camera details, lighting, composition, subject posture, texture, and mood. It also explains how to iterate with image edits instead of regenerating from scratch, which saves time and preserves consistency. For anyone working in visual design, social media content, storytelling, or brand imagery, this guide reveals how modern image models actually think and interpret instructions.

6. Veo Prompting Guide (Google / Vertex AI)

Google's Veo Prompting Guide is the definitive introduction to text-to-video prompting for Veo, Google's high-end generative video model. It explains how to structure prompts like a director: define the camera angle, shot duration, motion, lighting, scene transitions, and emotional tone. It walks you through combining text prompts with reference images to maintain character consistency across frames. This guide is priceless for creators, marketers, and video teams who want to use AI to produce cinematic clips with professional clarity.

7. ChatGPT-5 Prompting Guide

The ChatGPT-5 guide explains new features such as deeper reasoning modes, expanded context windows, and system-level instructions that allow granular control over how the model thinks and responds. It describes how to explicitly request "hard thinking," guide the model through multi-step reasoning, and embed constraints to produce more structured, accurate outputs. Anyone using ChatGPT professionally should study this, because it helps you extract maximum accuracy from one of the most advanced models currently available.

8. Research Playbook: "A Systematic Survey of Prompting Techniques"

This academic paper is one of the most rigorous and comprehensive surveys ever published on prompting. It categorizes more than fifty structured techniques, evaluates them across models, and explains when each method works, fails, or needs adaptation. The paper also introduces frameworks for measuring prompt quality using objective metrics. It is perfect for researchers, engineers, product teams, and anyone building reliable evaluation systems for prompts. If you want a deep scientific understanding of prompting, this is the gold standard.

9. Sora Prompting Guide (OpenAI)

The Sora guides explain how to write prompts that generate coherent cinematic video using OpenAI's Sora model. They emphasize writing prompts like a screenplay with clear scene descriptions, character actions, camera movement, pacing, and audio cues. You also learn how to use reference images, how to refine results through iterative adjustments, and how to navigate Sora-specific limitations. This guide is especially valuable for creators who want to produce short-form video narratives with consistency.

10. Copy-Paste Prompt Libraries

Copy-paste prompt libraries are community-driven collections of high-quality, ready-to-use prompts. These libraries give you templates for writing emails, creating summaries, analyzing research, planning projects, generating marketing content, and managing personal productivity. They are extremely practical because they provide instantly deployable prompts that you can modify for your specific use case. Over time, these templates help you develop your own library of customized prompts that reflect your workflow and style.

Scan the QR Code below & access the resources mentioned:

A Detailed 30-Day Learning Plan

If you want to become genuinely skilled at prompting, the most effective way is to follow a structured, month-long plan that progresses from fundamentals to practical application.

In the first week, focus entirely on the foundational concepts taught by OpenAI Academy and Learn Prompting. Spend time experimenting, testing variations, and writing down what worked and what didn't this builds your intuition faster than anything else.

In the second week, shift your attention to real-world workflows by exploring the role-based Prompt Packs offered by OpenAI. Choose a few prompts that match your profession or goals, run them multiple times, and analyze how small adjustments in tone, structure, or constraints change the output.

In the third week, dive into creative and multimodal models by studying the Nano Banana, Veo, and Sora guides. This is where you learn how images and videos interpret instructions differently from text, and you'll create both an image and a short clip to solidify your understanding.

In the final week, deepen your knowledge by reading the arXiv research playbook and applying its taxonomy to your own prompts. Build a personal library of prompts, record your best-performing variations, and begin treating prompt design as an iterative, testable craft.

By the end of thirty days, you will have a strong conceptual foundation, hands-on practice, and a repeatable workflow that makes you genuinely proficient at prompting.

Gemini API Quick Start

If you've ever wanted to combine Google's Gemini API with Next.js but felt unsure where to begin, this guide will walk you through everything step by step. Next.js is one of the most widely used React frameworks today, and it's perfect for beginners because it handles fast page loading, secure API routes, and easy deployment, all without complicated setup.

In this chapter, you'll learn how to turn prompts from earlier sections into real, interactive web applications. For example, you'll build features like uploading an image for Gemini to analyze and then displaying a Three.js visual effect based on that analysis. Even if you've never touched Next.js before, we'll start from scratch with simple explanations, copy-ready code, and clear instructions that feel like pair-programming with a mentor.

Along the way, you'll learn how to safely use environment variables, avoid common mistakes, and even add nice touches like streaming responses for a typewriter-style effect. By the end, you'll have created and deployed a complete app that can display results live all using Next.js and Gemini. This chapter is built for beginners and designed to help you confidently create your first fully functional AI-powered web application.

Q. What Is the Gemini API? Why Pair It with Next.js?

Let's start from the very beginning, without any technical confusion. Google's Gemini API is simply a tool that lets developers connect to Google's powerful AI models, the same kind that can understand text, analyze images, listen to audio, and even generate code or creative stories. It first launched in 2023 and became much faster and more capable by 2025. The best part is that it's available to everyone: you can use the free version of Gemini 1.5 Flash for quick tasks and testing, or upgrade to the Pro model if you ever need deeper reasoning or heavier workloads.

The free tier already gives you more than enough to experiment up to 15 requests per minute and around one million tokens a day perfect for building small apps, practicing prompts, or testing ideas from earlier chapters. Next.js, on the other hand, is a beginner-friendly framework built on top of React. Think of it as a smarter version of React that takes care of the difficult parts of building a website, like routing, handling server code, or connecting securely to APIs like Gemini.

When you use Gemini and Next.js together, they complement each other beautifully: Gemini creates the content or analysis, and Next.js displays it in a clean, dynamic way on a webpage. For example, you could enter a prompt, have Gemini describe it or generate code for a animation, and then let Next.js render that animation live in the browser. It's the perfect combination for beginners because you don't need to manage your own servers, and deployment is extremely easy services like Vercel even offer free hosting where pushing your code to Git automatically publishes your website. There are a few things to keep an eye on, like staying within Gemini's API limits or learning how Next.js handles routes, but we'll walk through all of that clearly. Before you start, just install Node.js (version 20 or above), run one simple command:

```
npx create-next-app@latest
```

and then follow the instructions (check the official doc) and start your development server with npm run dev. Within seconds, your new Next.js app will open in your browser at localhost:3000, ready for you to connect it to Gemini and build your first AI-powered project.

Getting Started: Setup, API Key, and Your First Next.js + Gemini "Hello"

Getting everything set up takes less time than making a cup of coffee, and there's absolutely no complicated steps or gatekeeping involved. To start, you'll need your Gemini API key. Just search for "Google AI Studio" and open the official site (ai.google.dev). Sign in with your Gmail account, click Get API Key, create a new key (you can name it something like "MyNextApp"), and copy the key. This key must stay private, so go to your Next.js project folder and create a file called .env.local, then paste your key inside as GOOGLE_API_KEY=yourkeyhere. This file is automatically ignored by Git, which keeps your key safe. Next, open your terminal inside your project and run:

```
npm install @google/genai
```

The package you just installed is the official Gemini SDK, which basically takes care of all the complex communication with Google's AI models for you, it's what allows your app to "talk" to Gemini without requiring any complicated setup or networking code. Now that it's installed, you're ready to build your first real test page.

Now for our test page, we'll name it Homeprompt & we'll start with the directive "use client"; which tells Next.js that this module must be rendered on the client (browser) so we can use browser features like useState and event handlers; immediately after we import useState from React, it gives us the ability to declare reactive stateful values that persist between renders.

```
import { useState } from "react";

export default function HomePrompt() {
  const [prompt, setPrompt] = useState("");
  const [response, setResponse] = useState("");
  const [loading, setLoading] = useState(false);
  const [error, seterror] = useState("");
```

Next we declare a default exported React functional component named HomePrompt, and inside it we declare four pieces of state using useState: prompt (a string holding the user's typed prompt), response (a string that will hold the text returned from your API), loading (a boolean used to disable controls and show progress while we wait), and error (a string used to show validation or network/ server errors). These four state hooks are the component's single source of truth for the UI and drive conditional rendering late.

The handleGenerate async function is the central action: it first guards against empty input by trimming prompt and, if empty, sets error to "Please enter a prompt" and returns early, this is client-side validation to avoid unnecessary network calls; after passing validation it clears previous errors and responses and flips loading to true so the UI can reflect the pending operation.

```
async function handleGenerate() {
if (!prompt.trim()) {
setError("Please enter a prompt");
return;
}

setError("");
setResponse("");
setLoading(true);
```

Inside the try block we call:

```
try {
      const res = await fetch("/api/gemini", {
        method: "POST",
        headers: { "Content-Type": "application/json" },
        body: JSON.stringify({ prompt }),
      });

      const data = await res.json();

      if (!res.ok) {
        setError(data?.error || `Server error (${res.status})`);
      } else {
        setResponse(data?.text ?? data?.error ?? "No response");
      }
    } catch (err: any) {
      console.error("Client fetch error:", err);
      setError("Network error – please try again");
    } finally {
      setLoading(false);
    }
```

The try section begins by sending a POST request to the /api/gemini endpoint using fetch, including JSON headers and a serialized body containing the user's prompt; the result is awaited and stored in res, after which the response is parsed with await res.json() and saved in data. Once the JSON is available, the code checks res.ok to determine whether the server returned a successful 2xx status: if it did not, it sets an error message using either data.error (if the server provided one) or a fallback string that includes the HTTP status code, giving clear and actionable feedback; if the request was successful, it updates the UI by setting response to data.text, or falls back to data.error or "No response" to avoid rendering undefined values.

The catch block handles unexpected problems (such as the user losing internet connection or the API route failing before returning a JSON response), logs the raw error to the console for debugging, and sets a clean, user-friendly message instructing them to try again. Finally, the finally block ensures that loading is always set back to false regardless of success or failure, so the UI including buttons, spinners, and disabled states returns to normal after the request cycle completes.

```
return (
    <div className="p-8 max-w-2xl mx-auto">
      <h1 className="text-2xl font-bold mb-4">Gemini + Next.js</h1>

      <textarea
        value={prompt}
        onChange={(e) => setPrompt(e.target.value)}
        placeholder="e.g., Tell me a fun fact about 2025 AI"
        rows={4}
        className="w-full p-3 border rounded mb-3 bg-white/5 text-white"
      />

      <div className="flex gap-2">
        <button
          onClick={handleGenerate}
          disabled={loading}
          className="bg-blue-600 text-white px-4 py-2 rounded disabled:opacity-50"
        >
          {loading ? "Generating…" : "Generate"}
        </button>
```

The returned JSX begins with a container that centers the UI, limits the maximum width, and adds comfortable padding around the content; inside it, an <h1> element with bold styling provides the page title. Below the heading, a controlled <textarea> is rendered, where its value is bound to the prompt state, and onChange updates that state as the user types, keeping React fully in control of the displayed input; it includes a placeholder to guide users, a fixed height of four rows, and Tailwind classes that give it full width, padding, a subtle border, rounded edges, spacing below, and a translucent dark-theme appearance with white text.

The action buttons are grouped inside a horizontally aligned <div className="flex gap-2">, providing spacing between them: the primary Generate button triggers handleGenerate when clicked, respects the loading state by disabling itself while a request is in progress, and updates its label to either "Generating…" or "Generate" to communicate real-time activity to the user.

```
<button
          onClick={() => {
            setPrompt("");
            setResponse("");
            setError("");
          }}
          className="px-4 py-2 border rounded text-white/80"
        >
          Clear
        </button>
      </div>

      {error && <div className="mt-4 text-red-400">{error}</div>}

      {response && (
        <div className="mt-6 p-4 bg-white/5 rounded whitespace-pre-wrap">
          {response}
        </div>
      )}
    </div>
  );
}
```

Next to it, the Clear button quickly resets the UI by clearing prompt, response, and error through a simple inline onClick handler, and its styling (px-4 py-2 border rounded text-white/80) gives it a clean, subtle secondary-button appearance. Below the buttons, the component conditionally renders any existing error message inside a red-styled container so issues like validation or server failures are immediately visible. Similarly, if a response exists, it is shown inside a styled block that maintains spacing, uses a dark translucent background, and includes whitespace-pre-wrap to preserve line breaks from the AI output, ensuring multi-line results display cleanly and accurately.

With this final section of the UI rendered, the component completes a clean, functional frontend for interacting with your Gemini-powered API, and the combination of a controlled textarea, responsive action buttons, clear error handling, and a neatly formatted response output gives you a solid, production-ready foundation. At this point, you've successfully created a basic Gemini API application that sends prompts, receives model-generated responses, and displays them in a polished, easy-to-use interface meaning you can now freely experiment with different prompts, test ideas, and explore how Gemini reacts to various inputs.

Below is an example of what the final page output typically looks like after entering a prompt and receiving a response, demonstrating the complete flow from input to result.

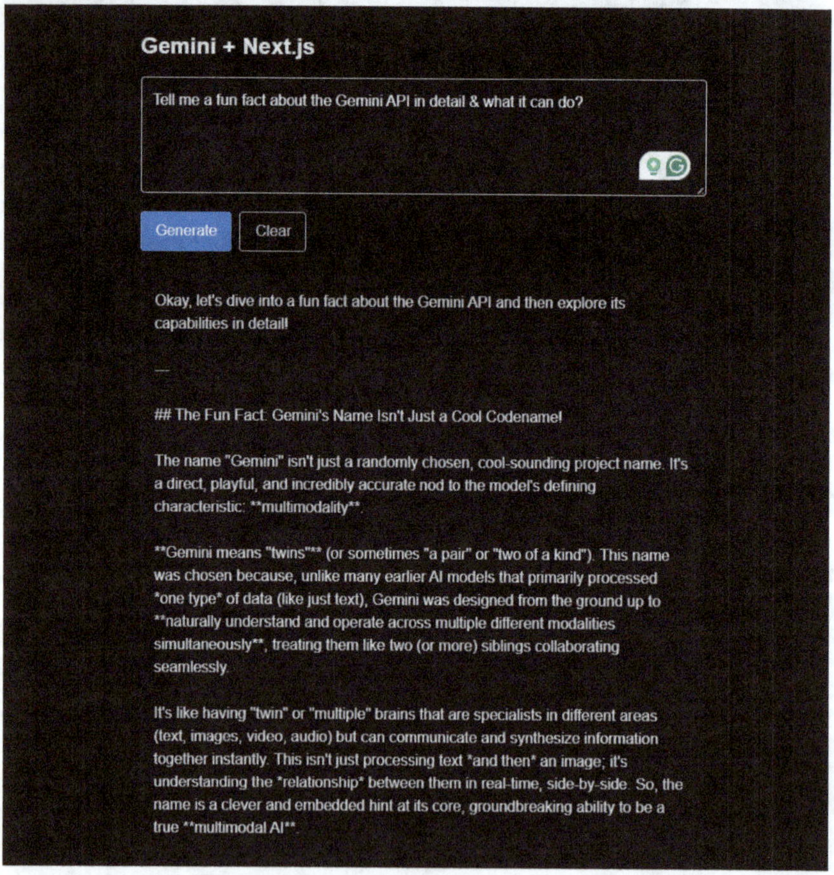

If you'd like the full source code, simply scan the QR code below.

NOTE: Once you access the ZIP folder, extract it, open the project, run npm install (or npm i) and make sure to insert your own API key before running the application. This step is essential for proper functionality and successful execution.

Model Comparison Table

(Gemini vs ChatGPT vs Claude vs Llama)

You must know, not all LLMs are created equal. Differences in architecture, training data, design goals, and optimization strategies mean that each model tends to excel in some areas and lag in others.

Understanding these differences becomes especially important if you're new to AI: what works best for creative writing may not work best for code generation; what works for short chats may falter on long documents; what's ideal for factual research may not be ideal for expressive style. The table and discussion below aim to clarify, in human terms, how ChatGPT, Google Gemini, Claude, and Llama compare (as of late 2025), and help you choose which one might fit your needs depending on what you want to achieve.

Comparison Table:

ChatGPT vs Gemini vs Claude vs Llama

Model / Feature	ChatGPT	Google Gemini	Claude	Llama
Context-window / Long-document memory	128,000 tokens (in "pro / top" versions)	Up to 1,000,000 tokens (or more, per some reports)	Near 200,000 tokens (or more in premium variants)	Varies (less than dedicated "long-context" models); typically more limited than Gemini/ Claude
General knowledge, reasoning & multi-task performance	Top-tier performance on many standard benchmarks, especially tasks requiring balanced reasoning + versatility	Highly competitive especially in knowledge, logic, translation, and tasks benefiting from long context or integration with Google ecosystem	Strong in structured reasoning, stable output style, and tasks requiring ethical / nuanced reasoning; consistent performance across many domains	Growing rapidly; open-source nature and adaptability make it attractive for custom and privacy-sensitive applications; performs decently for many standard tasks

Coding / Software & Data-Science Support	Good support overall, especially for general programming tasks debugging, explanations, cross-language help	Very good for structured tasks, especially when long context or integration with external data helps; suitable for code + documentation + large projects	Known to perform well on coding challenges / code generation tasks according to several benchmarks; often praised for reliability and comprehensiveness in code output	Can be suitable for coding in contexts where open-source, privacy, or customization matters. Performance is more variable compared to mainstream proprietary mo
Writing style, creativity, and expressive tasks	Very strong, especially for conversational, expressive, or creative writing, marketing copy, storytelling, explanatory prose, etc.	Solid. Tends to produce fact-driven, neutral, structured writing; maybe less flamboyant creatively but very good for technical / factual writing and documentation	Great at formal, nuanced, and detailed writing often excels in business / professional / legal / research-style outputs. Balanced between clarity and accountability.	More straightforward and "to-the-point." Good for plain technical or writing, but may lack polish compared to proprietary models.

Integration with tools / ecosystem & features	Strong ecosystem: plugins, browsing, extensions, widely used. Makes it versatile for many workflows.	Especially strong if you are already in the Google ecosystem (Search, Docs, Gmail, Drive, etc.) Offers tight integration and value for those workflows.	Good for enterprise-style workflows, privacy-oriented tasks, structured document analysis, and applications needing consistency and reliability.	As an open-source model, offers flexibility. Good if you want to self-host or fine-tune for custom uses, or prioritize privacy / cost control.

Detailed Observations & Guidance (When to Use Which)

1. When to pick ChatGPT?

ChatGPT is an excellent choice when you need balanced, all-around performance, strong general knowledge, reliable coding support, and high-quality creative writing. It particularly shines in expressive or imaginative tasks such as crafting marketing copy, developing narratives, building conversational assistants, and producing clear educational content. Its extensive ecosystem of plugins, tools, and community resources also makes it ideal for users who value flexibility and integration. Overall, ChatGPT performs best for typical everyday work where documents are moderate in length, such as essays, articles, and code snippets.

2. When Gemini shines?

Gemini excels when working with extensive content, long documents, full manuscripts, large codebases, or complex research datasets. Thanks to its significantly larger context window, which reduces the need to break material into smaller parts. It is especially effective for users who are deeply integrated into the Google ecosystem, including Docs, Drive, Gmail, and Search, as it streamlines workflows across these tools. Gemini is also well-suited for producing consistent, factual, and well-structured outputs, making it ideal for technical documentation, reports, research summaries, and translations. Overall, it is a strong choice for users who prioritize scalability, large-context reasoning, and seamless integration with real-world data and tools.

3. When Claude is the smart pick!

Claude is particularly well-suited for professional, formal, or nuanced writing tasks, such as legal documents, research summaries, business communications, and technical documentation. It also performs strongly in coding and data-science workflows where reliability, stability, and precision are essential. Known for its reduced tendency to "hallucinate", Claude generally delivers more cautious, well-reasoned responses. It is an excellent choice for users who prioritize alignment, clarity, structured reasoning, and consistent performance, especially during complex, multi-step analyses or tasks requiring deep, methodical thinking.

4. When Llama makes sense

Llama is an excellent choice when you prioritize open-source flexibility, transparency, privacy, and the ability to customize or self-host your models. It works particularly well for straightforward tasks such as plain technical writing, generating code for smaller projects, and rapid prototyping. Llama is also ideal in scenarios where cost efficiency, environmental control, or data governance are more important than achieving absolute state-of-the-art performance.

A Few Caveats & What "Stats" Mean. Why There's No "Perfect" Model?

Understanding the limitations of large language models requires looking beyond surface-level statistics such as benchmark scores, context windows, and coding accuracy, because these metrics rarely capture real-world performance. Benchmarks including reasoning tests, coding evaluations, and MMLU offers only a rough indication of capability; many test sets are publicly available and may already be represented in training data, which inflates scores and leads to "teaching to the test." Real tasks are far more complex, combining reasoning, long-range context, domain expertise, and stylistic nuance in ways that synthetic benchmarks cannot simulate.

Similarly, while a model's "context window" represents how much text it can process at one time, a larger window does not ensure perfect comprehension. Models often compress long inputs internally, causing reasoning degradation, retrieval fragility, and loss of detail long before reaching theoretical token limits. Even with expanded context sizes in modern systems, coherence across long documents, codebases, or research papers depends heavily on a model's attention mechanisms and internal heuristics, not just raw token capacity.

Coding benchmarks have similar limitations: they typically focus on small, self-contained tasks, while real-world software development involves ambiguous requirements, intricate dependency chains, domain-specific libraries, environment configuration, performance constraints, and error handling that benchmarks simply do not reflect. As a result, high benchmark accuracy does not guarantee reliable integration or production-ready code without human oversight. Moreover, these models evolve continuously. New versions often shift strengths, weaknesses, and trade-offs, while emerging research highlights deeper theoretical limits such as inherent hallucination tendencies, reasoning fragility, and persistent difficulty with complex, multi-step spatial or logical problems. Larger models and bigger context windows help, but scaling is not a universal solution; improved reasoning often comes at the cost of slower inference, higher compute requirements, and increased complexity.

Ultimately, no single model is "perfect." Each represents a different balance of power, efficiency, cost, reliability, and suitability for specific tasks. This is why hands-on testing with real data, combined with human review & domain knowledge, remains essential when evaluating or deploying any modern AI system.

Q. What's Best For You (Given a Beginner / Intermediate Use Case)

If you're just getting started with AI and want a tool that feels approachable, versatile, and helpful across a wide range of everyday tasks like writing, brainstorming ideas, learning new topics, or generating quick code snippets, ChatGPT is often the most comfortable and well-rounded choice. It offers a friendly user experience, strong creative abilities, and an extensive ecosystem that makes it easy to grow as you experiment.

If your work involves long-form content, such as research papers, e-books, technical archives, or large codebases and you want smooth integration with Google tools like Docs, Drive, and Search, Gemini can be a better fit. Its large context window and deep Google ecosystem alignment make it especially useful for handling big inputs and productivity workflows.

If your priority is reliability, precision, and professional-grade output, especially for formal writing, structured reasoning, business communication, or accurate code generation, Claude stands out. It tends to produce careful, well-reasoned responses with fewer errors, making it ideal for users who need clarity and consistency.

And if you value openness, control, privacy, or the ability to customize and self-host your tools, Llama provides the flexibility you need. While its performance can vary depending on the setup, it gives you more ownership of your environment, making it a strong option for users who prefer transparency or want to build tailored AI workflows.

Overall, the best model depends on your style, your goals, and how much control you want, each one shines in a different way.

Conclusion

1. How to Continue Improving Your Prompting Skills?

If you've started exploring AI tools like Grok, ChatGPT, or Claude, you've probably noticed something important, the real power comes from how you ask. Your prompt isn't just a message; it's the instruction manual you hand to a very smart but very literal assistant. When your prompt is clear and thoughtful, the AI can give you answers, ideas, and solutions that feel almost magical. But if your prompt is vague, the results can wander off track or feel irrelevant.

Prompting has quickly evolved from a quirky trick into a real skill almost like a new kind of digital literacy. And the best part? You don't need to be an expert to start. No jargon, no overcomplication, just simple, helpful advice to help you go from beginner to confident pro, one step at a time.

Step 1: Nail the Fundamentals: What Even Is a "Good" Prompt?

Before leveling up, it's important to understand what makes a prompt effective. Prompting is essentially the art of shaping your input so the AI can give you exactly the output you want. It isn't about fancy words; it's about being clear, specific, and intentional.

For starters, vague requests like "Tell me about history" usually lead to long, random responses that miss the point. But a prompt like "Give me a 300-word story-style summary of the key events in World War II, focused on the European theater, written for a 12-year-old" gives the AI a strong framework to follow. That's the power of specificity.

To get better fast, internalize a few key principles: keep your wording clear, provide background or context where needed, structure your request using roles or steps, and set constraints such as tone or length. A simple rule of thumb is this: if a prompt sounds confusing when you read it aloud, it will confuse the AI too.

Step 2: Build a Toolkit of Techniques: From Basic to Boss-Level

Improvement comes from practicing techniques that help the AI understand your goals more precisely. One of the easiest is role-playing, where you assign the AI a persona, such as "You are a career coach with 10 years at Google," so the answer automatically aligns with that expertise.

Another powerful approach is Chain of Thought prompting, where you tell the AI to "think step-by-step" before giving its final answer. This dramatically improves reasoning and decision-making tasks. You can also refine answers by treating the chat like a conversation instead of a one-shot request, ask follow-up questions, request expansions, or adjust the tone. Few-shot prompting is another excellent technique where you share one or two examples so the AI can imitate the pattern or style you want.

For tricky tasks, few-shot often outperforms simple instructions. As you practice, you'll learn when to use zero-shot prompts (no examples) and when to guide the AI with examples for a more accurate result.

Step 3: Practice Like a Pro: Daily Habits to Wire Your Brain

Like any skill, prompting gets sharper with daily practice. You don't need hours, ten minutes a day is enough to build strong prompting instincts. Try keeping a prompt journal where you save your prompts, the AI's responses, what worked, and how you improved it. Theme days help too: role-play experiments on Mondays, reasoning prompts on Wednesdays, and creative challenges on Fridays.

Once a week, revisit old prompts and compare how much better your new results are, that's the quickest way to measure progress. Join beginner-friendly communities on Reddit or Discord, where you can share prompts, ask questions, and see how others solve similar tasks. These interactions help you grow faster and keep your ideas fresh.

Step 4: Dodge the Pitfalls: Common Beginner Traps and Fixes

Even experienced users make mistakes, so it's helpful to know the common traps early. One big one is overloading the prompt with too much information, long, cluttered prompts confuse the AI. Keep your initial request under 200 words and expand only if needed. Another issue is forgetting to set tone or check for bias; simply stating "neutral and evidence-based" or "respectful and humorous" can completely change the output. Many beginners also forget to iterate one follow-up message can improve an answer more than rewriting your entire prompt. Finally, avoid limiting yourself to one AI. Each model has its own strengths: Grok is great for witty, punchy responses, Claude excels at depth and structure, and ChatGPT is a balanced all-rounder. Testing across multiple models sharpens your intuition and exposes you to better patterns.

Step 5: Resources to Fuel Your Journey: Where to Learn More

You're not alone in this journey, there are plenty of free resources to help you keep improving. OpenAI and Anthropic both offer simple, beginner-friendly prompt guides and template libraries. If you want deeper hands-on practice, check out books like The Prompt Engineering Guide by DAIR.AI or Prompt Engineering for Generative AI by James Phoenix. Tools like Grok's free interface or PromptBase give you places to experiment and explore ideas.

You can also learn visually through YouTube tutorials and podcasts such as "The AI Breakdown", which explain prompting concepts in quick, digestible ways. Since AI evolves rapidly, revisiting resources each month helps you stay up to date with new techniques, especially as multimodal prompts using images or audio become more common.

2. The Future of AI Prompt Engineering

I've always thought of prompt engineering as a kind of modern sorcery: the right arrangement of words can conjure vivid stories, razor-sharp analyses, or laugh-out-loud comedy. Prompt engineering isn't a quirky hobby for a handful of power users; it's the interface between human intent and machine capability. As AI becomes as omnipresent as the smartphone, it's worth asking: where is this bridge taking us?

Below I offer an honest projection of prompt engineering's trajectory, no corporate gloss, just patterns I've observed, a few tradeoffs, and a healthy dose of optimism. I'll cover the weaknesses we're bumping into today, the innovations that are bubbling up, and what I think the next decade will bring. Buckle up.

The fragile art we're working with today

Right now, prompt engineering is part art, part science and, if I'm honest, mostly art. It's the craft of composing inputs that coax useful, accurate, or creative outputs from large language models. The best prompts layer context, constrain format, anticipate bias, and build in safety. The worst? A few ambiguous words or a misplaced comma and the result can go badly off-track. I've seen people spend hours iterating just to get an extra table, a different tone, or a minor structural change. That brittleness matters.

In the short term it forces us to be mindful about language, intent, and ethics. Long term, it's unsustainable. We can't expect every analyst, teacher, or artist to become expert prompt mechanics. If AI is going to scale, the way we interact with it must evolve. Broadly, I see that evolution happening across three waves: automation, hybridization, and humanization.

Wave One - Automation: prompts that write themselves

Imagine it's 2030 and you no longer grind over prompt tweaks. Instead you talk to a "prompt optimizer" , a meta-AI that translates a loose idea like "Help me plan a sustainable garden" into a hyper-tuned prompt for the core model. This is already emerging: systems that treat prompts like code, make them testable, and iteratively optimize them. Variants of models that self-refine prompts on the fly will reduce hallucinations and shorten the iterate-test cycle.

This automation democratizes access. A student in a remote village could get a personalized tutor as easily as a coder in Silicon Valley. For practitioners, it feels like upgrading from a typewriter to a full editor: more power, less friction. But there are risks. Over-reliance on optimizers can silently propagate biases present in their training data. The antidote is transparency, open audits, and community governance open models and clear evaluation pipelines so anyone can inspect how optimizers make decisions.

Wave Two - Hybridization: prompts as part of an AI ecosystem

Prompts won't remain isolated. They'll be one component in a broader orchestration of fine-tuning, retrieval-augmented generation, agents, and multimodal inputs. We already see early agents that break tasks into subprompts, use tools, and iterate. The future likely holds visual "prompt graphs", drag-and-drop workflows that link prompt nodes to databases, sensors, and other models.

Combine that with multimodality and you get powerful new workflows: "Enhance this sketch into a 3D model, then simulate wind flow," or "Analyze satellite feeds, merge with economic indicators, and forecast drought impacts." Prompt engineering will shift toward system design and pipeline thinking: how different components interact to serve a high-level intent. That shift makes AI feel less like a chatbot and more like a collaborator. But it also raises questions about access and equity. If these orchestration platforms are gated behind paywalls, power will concentrate. Open, interoperable tooling is therefore essential to keep this innovation broadly beneficial.

Wave Three - Humanization: intuitive, ethical, and delightful prompting

The most exciting wave is not technical complexity, but humanity. Prompt engineering won't just become easier, it will become more natural. Interfaces will understand context, intent, and emotion. A model might detect you're rushed and summarize with bullet points, or recognize cultural idioms and reframe them for a global audience. Interaction design will absorb prompting, turning it into conversational design: an ongoing, two-way collaboration where the model suggests refinements like a skilled editor.

This humanization opens creative possibilities. Prompting can be playful, gamified experiences, collaborative storytelling, or co-creative tools that make exploration joyful rather than tedious. That said, new capabilities bring new harms. Sophisticated prompts can craft highly convincing deepfakes or hyper-targeted manipulation. So we must embed "prompt hygiene": transparency logs, bias detectors, user consent mechanisms, and norms that prioritize truth and dignity. Those safeguards are not optional; they're foundational.

Q. Where does that leave us?

Prompt engineering's future will be bright, messy, and profoundly human. It will automate the grunt work, blend into complex AI ecosystems, and become more intuitive but it will also demand new literacies: systems thinking, ethics, and collaborative design. For creators and users alike, the liberation is that we'll spend less time on syntax and more time on intent.

My final thought: don't mourn the decline of manual prompt tinkering. Treat it as a transition from mechanics to meaning. The real magic was never in exact phrasing alone; it's in curiosity, context, and purpose. Whatever tools arrive, they should amplify that spark. Prompt boldly and help build an AI future that's not only smart, but also soulful.

Connect with me

Thank you for taking the time to read this book. I truly appreciate your curiosity, dedication, and interest in exploring creative technology. Your support enables me to continue building meaningful projects, writing new books, and sharing resources that help developers, designers, and creators bring their ideas to life. If you'd like to dive deeper into my work, discover upcoming projects, or follow along with my latest releases, I've made it easy for you to stay connected.

The QR code on this page lead directly to my LinkedIn, where you'll find tutorials, announcements, and exclusive content available. And if you ever want to talk, collaborate, or ask questions in real time, I'm always open to connecting personally. If you'd like to hop on a Zoom call, just reach out to me on LinkedIn, and I'll be happy to schedule a session.

Explore my Other Books

Make sure you don't miss a thing!

References

1. **FlowGPT:** https://flowgpt.com

2. **Learning Prompt:** https://learnprompting.org

3. **Prompting Guide (PromptEngineering Guide)**
https://www.promptingguide.ai

4. **Awesome ChatGPT Prompts (GitHub)**
https://github.com/f/awesome-chatgpt-prompts

5. **OpenAI Prompt Engineering Guide:**
https://platform.openai.com/docs/guides/prompt-engineering

6. **Cohere Prompting Guide:**
https://docs.cohere.com/docs/prompt-engineering

7. **Llama Prompting Guide (Meta)**
https://llama.meta.com/docs/how-to-guides/prompting/

8. **PromptPerfect (Free Trial / Free Tier Available)**
https://promptperfect.jina.ai

9. **Krea AI (Free Tier):** https://www.krea.ai

10. **Lexica - Prompt Explorer for AI Images:** https://lexica.art

11. **PromptLayer (Free Tier)**
https://promptlayer.com

12. **OpenPrompt (Open-Source Prompt Framework)**
https://github.com/thunlp/OpenPrompt

13. **PromptSource (Dataset of Prompt Templates by BIG-bench Authors)**
https://github.com/bigscience-workshop/promptsource

14. **Microsoft Guidance (Open-Source Prompting Framework)**
https://github.com/microsoft/guidance

15. DSPy - Declarative Self-improving Python (Stanford, Open Source): https://github.com/stanfordnlp/dspy

16. FlowiseAI - Open-Source Prompt & Agent Builder: https://flowiseai.com/

17. Agenta - Open-Source Prompt Management: https://agenta.ai/

18. GrammarlyGO: https://www.grammarly.com/ai

19. TabAI Summarizer: https://tabai.dev/

20. Github Copilot: https://github.com/features/copilot

21. Cursor AI: https://cursor.com/

22. ReplitAI: https://replit.com/ai?gad_campaignid=23286661337

23. OpenAI Academy: https://academy.openai.com/public/clubs/work-users-ynjqu/resources/prompting

24. Google/Gemini Prompting Guide: https://services.google.com/fh/files/misc/gemini-for-google-workspace-prompting-guide-101.pdf

25. Anthropic Academy: https://www.anthropic.com/learn

26. Learn Prompting ("How to Prompt"): https://learnprompting.org/docs/introduction

27. Nano Banana Prompting Guide: https://blog.google/products/gemini/prompting-tips-nano-banana-pro/

28. Veo Prompting Guide (Google / Vertex AI): https://docs.cloud.google.com/vertex-ai/generative-ai/docs/video/video-gen-prompt-guide

29. ChatGPT-5 Guide: https://openai.com/index/introducing-gpt-5/

30. Research Playbook: Prompting Techniques (arXiv): https://arxiv.org/abs/2406.06608

31. Sora Prompting Guide: https://help.openai.com/en/articles/12456897-getting-started-with-the-sora-app

32. Copy-Paste Prompt Libraries: https://www.aiprm.com/prompts/

www.ingramcontent.com/pod-product-compliance
Lightning Source LLC
Chambersburg PA
CBHW062106160726
48282CB00026B/686
9789334391213